Retriever Training
for the
Duck Hunter

Robert Milner

SAFARI PRESS, Inc.

Milner, Robert.

ISBN 940143-90-9

1993, Long Beach, California, U.S.A.

10 9 8 7 6 5 4 3 2

Readers wishing to receive the Safari Press catalog, featuring many fine
books on big-game hunting, wingshooting, and firearms should write the
publisher at the address given above.

This is the 49th book published by Safari Press.

CONTENTS

Portions of this book have previously appeared in *Water-fowler's World Magazine*.

Young Derby Dog—
"Flyin' To Go"
Owner: Pam Bird

FOREWORD

There is a Boykin Spaniel named Pistol sitting at my feet, staring at me with liquid eyes, who owes a lot to Bob Milner. As a matter of fact, we both do.

I met Bob in the summer of '81. He was vacationing in Montana, and a mutual friend had suggested that we get to know each other. Bob was writing a book on dog training, and I was in need of a retriever to eventually fill in for my older Lab. I was also the world's worst dog handler; they tended to train me, rather than the other way around.

It seemed a perfect meeting. I might be able to trade some advice regarding book contracts, form and promotion, for his suggestions regarding a dog and a reputable breeder and trainer. I had long given up any hopes of turning a pup into a polished hunter on my own.

As our front porch conversation progressed, primed by a soft mountain evening and occasional sips of Jack Daniels, it became clear that mine was the greater luck. Bob had a firm handle on the business of book writing, so the advice he needed from me was minimal. Bob, however, was also a professional breeder and trainer; an ideal and immediate source of reliable information.

I outlined my basic needs in a hunting partner; an all-around flushing dog and retriever that travelled well. In the course of a season, I normally hunt grouse, pheasant, waterfowl, quail, and dove from Montana to Mexico. Labs, thus far, had proven the most workable choice, although they didn't take the heat well, and took up a lot of leg room in the cab of a pickup.

"Did you ever consider a Boykin Spaniel," Bob asked?

I had heard of the breed, but just in passing. When Bob outlined their traits; small, devoted, fast to learn and fiercely determined, they sounded ideally suited to my purpose. What's more, he had a bitch Boykin who had just whelped that day.

"You've got me convinced," I allowed halfway through the evening. "Send me one of those pups, but I want you to train it."

"Why spend all that money?" Bob asked, puzzled. "Train him yourself...it's easy."

"Whoa!" I countered, and proceeded to list my failures; the Brittainy who hunted by herself, her daughter, who had me convinced she was stone deaf because she wouldn't respond to my commands, the Lab who broke as birds tolled to the blocks and long before they ever reached gunrange...

Bob just smiled, and then struck a rare bargain that would be something of a test for both of us. He would send me chapters from his book as they were completed. If I followed the text, and still had difficulty in getting the predicted response, he would then train the dog.

Pistol arrived in our house that fall, and what unfolded thereafter was astounding to this full time writer and part time, fumble-fingered trainer. By verse and chapter, the little dog learned obedience; to sit, to kennel, to come when called, even when preoccupied with the wonders of a dead songbird or mouse nest. Then later, he learned to retrieve, first single dummies thrown a few feet, then doubles, triples, even blind retrieves, tossed as far as my arm could hurl them.

The real test occurred in October of '82, during the first week of duck season. Four of us spent two days up at the lake, bagging over 30 birds. It was Pistol's first exposure to real hunting conditions, and he performed flawlessly, retrieving not just stone dead easy marks, but lively cripples on water, and birds that hit land and burrowed into cattails. When I chanted "dead-dead" he became a creature obsessed. He followed hand and mouth commands by the numbers. Not one bird was lost. Needless to say, I was convinced of the value of Bob's book.

But there is another dimension to this work that unfolded with each chapter; a practical and readable approach to training and obedience that is as responsible for its success as the hard facts of repetition and conditioning. It is packed with disarmingly cogent advice.

On choosing a puppy;
.... There is no such thing as the "pick of the litter." Three or four generations of bloodlines will tell you more of a dog's potential than immediate characteristics of a green pup. Just make sure he comes from good hunting stock, and pick the pup that appeals to you.

On raising a puppy;
.... Raise him in the house, not in a kennel. He needs all the love and play time you can give him. He needs to be exposed to sights, sounds and smells to make him inquisitive and bold. A bond will thus develop between the two of you.

drawing
"Puppy Golden
Retriever"
"Bandit"

On training a young dog;

    .... Most problems encountered are people problems, not dog problems.... Beware of "magic" trainers with overnight solutions to undesirable patterns of behavior.

Even humor blends with how-to; ...A pinch collar, placed just behind the ears, will allow your grandmother to control a great dane of equivalent weight.. When introducing a pup to real birds, one of three things will happen. He will ignore it, he will pick it up and bring it to you, or he will drag it into the bushes and eat it. People over react to a dog eating birds. It's much easier to teach a dog not to eat birds than to teach him to like retrieving them. Among its many other credentials, the book is fun to read.

But most important, I think, is a philosophy that emerges with each page turned; a humanistic approach to dog training that dispells myths and encourages a partnership between you and your hunting companion. Above all else, Bob Milner cares about people and he cares about their dogs, and it shows in the end product of his education. Looking back at that curly, chocolate bundle of energy and devotion at my feet, I can only ask "what better way?"

Norman Strung

"The Great Masking Tape Robbery~"
9 weeks old—
"Diamond in The Ruff"

Dixie Mallard —
in honor of Richard Bishop
and
Edgar M. Queeny

DEDICATION

This book is dedicated to Ducks Unlimited, and to all it's members, without whom there probably would be no need to write about this subject. For without DU we would without a doubt be severely lacking in ducks to hunt. DU's unswerving dedication to the conservation of waterfowl is preserving for future generations this beautiful and unique facet of the great outdoors. We should not forget that their efforts are affording us our present day opportunities to pursue the pastime of waterfowling.

Through this book, I hope to provide you the opportunity to make a small contribution toward our mutual goal of waterfowl conservation, while at the same time adding the richness arising from the pleasurable companionship of a well trained working duck dog. A well trained retriever is a direct and visible contributor to waterfowl conservation. From my experience, I would estimate that the average duck hunter successfully retrieves 75% of the ducks he knocks down. That same hunter with a well trained retriever would take home at least 95% of those ducks. This is a direct contribution to conservation, and one of which any duck hunter can be justifiably proud.

What this 20% figure would translate into in terms of equivalent production from purchased or developed breeding areas is hard to say. However, if every duck hunter used a trained retriever, that 20% conservation measure would be equal in effect to DU's purchasing a substantial amount of wetland propagation area. It is with this understanding that I ask you to approach your training program with seriousness of purpose and diligence, knowing that you're doing your extra bit for conservation.

BIOGRAPHICAL SKETCH

Robert Milner graduated from Memphis State University in 1967 with a B.S. in Mathematics. Upon graduation, he served five years in the USAF. He's currently a Major in the Air Force Reserve serving as a Disaster Preparedness Augmentation Officer at Columbus AFB, Mississippi, and additionally as an Admissions Liaison Officer for the USAF Academy and ROTC.

After separating from active duty in 1972, he converted a hobby into a business by starting a dog training kennel in Grand Junction, Tenn., where he is actively engaged in training retrievers for hunting and for field trials. He enjoys a national reputation and is well known on the field trial circuit. Additionally, for the past five years, he has taught dog obedience classes at Memphis State University.

His more than 20 years experience in dog training is added to his sheer enjoyment of the challenges in teaching novice dog owners "how to do it themselves." This has resulted in a book which will teach anyone to train his dog. Milner tells you how to train all of them, not just the "textbook models."

yellow lab with
"Cock" Pheasant—

The Big Honker

INTRODUCTION

This book is written for the duck hunter who has his first dog and very little experience or knowledge of how to go about the training of a duck dog. This four to six month training program is organized as a series of lessons which, if properly followed, will result in the molding of that dog into a truly effective and controllable hunting companion.

As a gun dog trainer of some years experience, I've accumulated some knowledge of the multitude of training problems which are generally encountered in dealing with the retriever. This training program is designed to anticipate and/or correct a great number of these problems. It is of particular interest to note that most of the problems encountered in a training program are owner created or caused. It is therefore important that you understand my interpretation of their causes so that you may, hopefully, avoid them.

There are many different ways to instill a desired behavior in a dog, but I have found this particular training program to be the most generally applicable to the largest portion of the retriever breeds. I have also found this program to be quite successful for implementation by the novice trainer.

Anyone can train a retriever.

Picking Puppies —

Chapter 1
Different Strokes for Different Pups

Let's begin with an understanding that dog training is easy and that anyone can do it. There are no magic tricks necessary to train a dog. All it takes is looking at it from a pup's point of view, a little common sense, and being consistent. The objective of this book is to show you how to train your dog in daily sessions of 5 to 15 minutes, and do most of it in your backyard or garage.

We will train your dog together, in a step by step structured and graduated program. The biggest problem that you, as trainer, will encounter is the "reading of your dog" and knowing "what to do when" so we'll devote this first chapter to dog personality types. This will enable you to place your dog in a certain category. By knowing this most important facet, you'll follow a series of specific training exercises; all of which you must modify to fit your dog's personality. By following this program, in 4 - 6 months you should have a responsive and obedient dog, who is steady to shot, proficient at double and triple marked retrieves, and has a good start on hand signals and blind retrieves.

You have heard some dogs referred to, sometimes vigorously, as "hard headed S.O.B.'s," "trained with a 2 x 4," "spooky as a snake," and worse. These terms of endearment refer to certain personality flaws which I will carefully explain, and I will teach you "how" to deal with these behavior types. Don't be discouraged. They are nearly all trainable. The only retrievers who aren't worth training are those who have little or no retrieving desire, those who aren't particularly interested in birds, and those who are physically injured and shouldn't be put through vigorous training. Most other problems, however, can be overcome. You must also accept the fact that some dogs will simply take a little longer to train than others, and our training program will help you identify these dogs. Your training schedules will be either extended or accordingly altered.

Another problem that you, as trainer, will have is reading your dog and knowing what level of conditioning to achieve.

You have now learned that all dogs are different. There is a great range of dog personalities and your training program must be adjusted to your own dog with his or her particular behavioral traits. What I'll do now is somewhat of a simplification, but, hopefully, we'll provide a few models, one of which ought to be similar to your own dog. We'll look at 5 different common personality traits of pups. These traits are: 1. Dominance, 2. Activeness, 3. Aggressiveness, 4. Responsiveness to people, and 5. Toughness. These categories may tend to overlap and not lend themselves to sharp delineation but, hopefully, will improve your frame of reference. These traits should be viewed in terms of greater degree of, some of, or may be toward the lesser degrees of the scale. Looking at these traits individually, we'll label both the upper and lower ends of the scale:

Food Pan and
Rawhide Chew—
a puppies favorite
Things—

1. Dominance vs Subordinance

Dogs are descended from wolves and retain some vestiges of wolf behavioral traits. Chief among these is dominance. In the wolf pack, there is a pecking order with the most dominant wolf being the leader, the next most dominant being second and so on down to the least dominant and therefore most subordinate. How does the boss wolf achieve and maintain this dominance? First, he's born with a genetic difference in dominance. The more dominant wolf maintains his position mostly by means of ritual behaviors rather than by fighting other wolves.

These behavior traits will be useful to us in training because, in order to get pup to obey you consistently, you must be dominant in relation to the pup. Some of the things we'll use to achieve dominance are a direct threatening stare, imposing posture, and petting or not. The petting is relative to dominance through its similarity to grooming. In the pack the leader is groomed by subordinates, but does not himself groom others. Similarly, a lot of petting tends to reinforce the dominance in a dominant dog. Conversely, a lot of petting is desirable for the dog of subordinate, submissive nature. A handy gauge for dominance is whether pup is jumping up on you. The dominant wolf will demonstrate his dominance by standing with his front feet on the shoulders

2

of or straddling the subordinate. Thus the dog who frequently jumps up and puts his paws on the handler should be telling you something. He's feeling dominant. Conversely, when properly trained, that same dog will not jump up even though he's never been corrected specifically for jumping on the handler.

Another facet of dominance which tends to suffer great abuse is the soliciting of affection from adult dogs. When a person solicits affection from a dog, he is performing in a manner similar to that of a wolf puppy's submissive behavior in the presence of the boss wolf. Thus you are tending to communicate submissiveness on *your* part to the adult dog.

In order to attain a dominant relationship with your pup, you must require responsiveness from him. The responsiveness is achieved by teaching pup behavioral patterns and requiring his compliance. The compliance is insured by conditioning the proper responses to the point that strong habits are formed. Then deviations from these habits are corrected. These deviations are frequently an expression on pup's part of a tendency to increase his dominance. Thus judicious, consistent correction of deviations tends to keep the balance of dominance where it belongs, with the handler.

To illustrate, one of your first control exercises for pup will be to teach him to heel. As you will discover in the obedience chapter, we will be teaching pup not only to heel but also to pay attention to the handler and keep himself at heel. We are placing the responsibility for maintaining proper position on pup's shoulders. Thus, in effect, we are requiring him to follow the handler. This is a great boost to enhancing handler dominance.

In like manner, much of our training program will be geared toward establishing and maintaining handler dominance. You don't want to expend all this effort building dominance on the one hand while tearing it down on the other hand with excessive petting and soliciting of affection. How much petting is optimum depends on pup's personality type. If you've got a dominant aggressive "hardhead" then very little petting is in order. Use verbal praise, the act of retrieving, and birds for this pup's reward. Conversely, the shy submissive type needs lots of petting and lots of verbal praise. With all types, during work sessions bestow the reward, be it petting or verbal praise, for successful completion of a desired behavior. Don't indiscriminately bestow praise according to whim and fancy. Keep in mind that reward, whatever its form, is a training tool and that misused petting can degrade your dominant position.

2. Aggressive vs. Inhibited

The aggressive dog is brave, curious, not afraid of new situations or places; while the inhibited dog is the reverse. Aggressiveness is desirable in your dog and makes him easier to train. However, the inhibited dog can usually be

Fast Pitch, anyone?
"— 8 week's Old —
Good Times Boss"

3

made more aggressive. The condition is often a result of lack of exposure to strange sights and sounds while pup was growing up. The solution is a lot of long walks in the city and in the fields and woods with consequent exposure to sights and sounds. This should be done before you start the shy dog's training program. *You can't train a frightened dog.* He will associate his feelings of fear with what you are trying to teach him, which will hardly result in an effective training session. Therefore, the inhibited dog's confidence should be reinforced *before the training program begins,* and his program should be geared to a slower pace than the more aggressive dog. Also a lot more birds are called for in his program to build up aggressiveness. Additionally, a lot of petting is called for in this pup's program. There is probably a lack of dominance associated with this pup. As we'll see in "Raising a Puppy" it's easier to raise a pup properly in the first place and thus avoid problems with a lack of aggressiveness.

3. Tough vs. Soft
Here we're simply talking about a dog's pain threshold. Some respond to the lightest touch and some initially take a pretty good whack. We'll use this information not for punishment, but for conditioning. Any force we use will be introduced lightly and gradually intensified to the point required for proper response. Also, any and all force will be used on a planned basis to develop conditioned responses. If we develop those responses well enough and *do not ask too much too soon from pup,* there should never occur a situation calling for punishment. However, the force that is used in conditioning programs must be proportionate to the dog's personality so keep this in mind.

4. Active vs. Lethargic
This refers to what some would call being "high strung." The upper end of the scale would be the hyperactive dog. He can't quit moving; he's always bounding around. At the other end is the dog who sleeps most of the time and moves slowly. This aspect of personality will determine the work schedule. The active dog could probably be worked 8 days a week with no problem. However, the lethargic dog needs much less, maybe three days a week, and lots of birds to keep his motivation high.

Actually the lethargic dog should be examined to see *why* he's under-active. Take him to your vet, and be certain it's not a physical problem. Confine him to his kennel when he's not working. When his only activity outlet is learning and retrieving, then his intensity is not dissipated in other areas. I've seen some young dogs who were lethargic simply because they were tired. They spent all their waking hours roaming the neighborhood, playing with children and dogs, and simply didn't have much energy left for work. Confining this type of dog, except during working periods, ought to dramatically improve his training performance by channeling all his energy into his work.

5. Sensitive vs. Unresponsive to People

The dog who is sensitive and responsive to people, who cares whether you're pleased with him or unhappy with him, is a pleasure to train for he responds to reward. At the other end of the stick, literally, is the dog who is unresponsive to people. As far as he's concerned, the trainer is not there. Reward in the form of petting or praise is meaningless to him. Therefore, more control must be used and other rewards must be found. If he's very birdy and loves retrieving, then these aids can be used, by granting or withholding, as rewards. However the unresponsive dog is going to be more difficult to train. He'll require a longer program with more intense conditioning and more control.

The personality categories which we have discussed are not all encompassing, but are meant to give you a simple framework upon which to build *your program for your dog.* Remember that what I've presented here are the extremes and most dogs will fall toward the middle of most of the categories, showing one trait a bit more or less than average.

One of the principle modifications you can make in adjustment to your dog's personality is that of increasing or decreasing the number of lessons. The most important parts of pup's training program are presented in a sequence of specific lessons. The number and duration of these lessons is geared to the average dog with a fairly inexperienced trainer. A totally inexperienced, first time trainer with a dominant, aggressive, and hyperactive dog would probably benefit by greatly increasing the number of lessons. Conversely, the trainer who is working on his third or fourth dog and has a relatively tractable dog could probably eliminate quite a few of the training sessions. As we go through the training program, we will discuss workable modifications that should be made for various behavioral types.

crowland
1988

7 week old puppy,
1st water Retrieve
"Music City's Jesse Jane
OWNER: La Donna Crowe

Lots of people contact is what a small puppy needs.

Personality —

Chapter 2
Puppies

Picking a Puppy — If you don't yet have a dog, let's digress from training for a moment and discuss an effective selection process. You'll be choosing a hunting partner who will be with you for the next eight to ten years, or more, so do it carefully; this is a fairly long term commitment. The wrong choice can make it downright unpleasant. The right one adds a whole new dimension to the enjoyment of hunting for you and your new dog.

First look at your type of hunting and its conditions. Are you primarily a duck hunter who hunts mostly on cold, rough coastal water, frequently in ice? Do you also hunt pheasants, and perhaps some doves? Take these factors into consideration when picking the breed. Some breeds are better than others with respect to different hunting conditions.

Looking first at the most numerous and most popular of the retrievers, you'll see the Labrador. This dog is overall the best bet for the average hunter. He's an excellent cold water dog who's not afraid to break ice to retrieve your ducks. He's also excellent on upland game, performing admirably as a flusher and retriever of pheasant. He's intelligent, relatively easy to train, and an excellent family member.

If you have problems with pup coming, simply run away. He'll chase you.

FC/AFC
Wild Fire of
River View -
Golden Retriever

Golden Retrievers have all the good attributes of Labs with one exception. The odds are a bit less on a Golden being a good cold water dog. They don't have the physical protection of a Lab for cold water work. The Golden lacks the oily, water-shedding outer coat of the Labrador. Thus he's going to get colder in icy water. That's not to say that there are not some Goldens around who are great cold water dogs. There are. However, the odds are not as good on a Golden turning out to be a good cold water dog as they are for a Labrador. The Golden is going to have to have more go-power and retrieving desire than the Lab to keep going back into that cold water because the Golden simply isn't dressed as warmly.

This brings us to the master of cold water and tough conditions: The Chesapeake Bay Retriever. He'll be diving back into the icy water long after the Labs and Goldens have called it quits. However, the Chessie does have some drawbacks. The Chesapeake has a strong protective instinct. He has a strong inclination to protect his yard, his car, his boat, his master, and his master's children. This is an admirable trait but it can also be inconvenient. What he perceives to be an intruder is not necessarily what we perceive as threatening. Suppose your kids are out playing and yelling and your neighbor walks over a little too fast, and a little too close to the children? This can cause a rapid decline in your popularity. Or suppose your hunting partner is too abrupt in his movement upon entering the boat? This can sink your popularity to even newer lows.

Again, I'm not saying that *all* Chesapeakes are this way, but a proportionately large number are, compared to the Labs and Goldens. I'm also not saying that this eliminates him as a choice for your hunting dog. I am saying that this protective trait needs to be recognized and that the owner must realize that the Chesapeake will require more supervision and control to avoid the type of situation where the dog is likely to bite what he perceives to be a threat.

Another consideration in your choice of Chesapeakes is that they tend to be difficult to train. They are difficult for all but the most experienced trainer to dominate, and respond poorly to force. Trainer communication with the dog is more demanding and these dogs seem to respond better to persuasion and much repetition, thus resulting in a considerably longer training program. I usually plan on double the duration of program for Chesapeake versus Lab or Golden.

In a discussion of duck dogs, I don't think the Boykin Spaniel should be left out of the conversation. This is a small brown dog of thirty to forty pounds and typically spaniel in appearance. The breed originated in South Carolina in the early 1800's and is currently recognized only by the Boykin Spaniel Society. The individual Boykins I've come in contact with have been very aggressive retrievers and quite easy to train. They make superb dove dogs, taking the heat quite well. They are also excellent water dogs, but they'll fall

Teach pup with play and food as rewards. Get pup to sit **and stay before he gets his supper.**

behind the Chesapeake and Lab when the going gets tough and there is ice to be broken. The Boykin lacks some of the physical protection for severe cold. Additionally, compared to the Lab, a Boykin's small size requires him to do about five times as much work to retrieve the same duck. However, this small size is ideal for boat hunting. He's not going to threaten you with imminent capsizing every time he leaves the boat. Thus, the Boykin would be a choice for the duck hunter who is operating in not too severe conditions. He does appear to have a small advantage over the larger breeds in tractability and ease of training.

With this brief treatment of the breeds, I'll leave the final analysis of your type of hunting conditions and consequent choice of breed to you.

The next problem is to pick the individual of that breed. The solution is not to pick the individual puppy, but to *pick the litter*. "Pick of the litter" is one of the most overworked terms in dogdom. If the litter is mediocre then no amount of "picking" is going to make the individual puppy better than mediocre. You've got to have the genes. So pick a good litter; then the odds are much better on the individual puppy turning out to be a good dog.

The way to pick a good litter is by knowing that the parents and grandparents are good working dogs. Now this information on ancestors tends to be a little hard to come by and at times difficult to verify, as some dog breeders may tend to inflate their descriptions of "Old Sport's" hunting prowess. So, in the absence of personal knowledge of the parents, one must go to the Pedigree to evaluate the promise of a litter. On the pedigree you want to see several titled ancestors in the first three generations, preferably on both the dam's and the sire's sides. The titles you are looking for are Field Champion or Amateur Field Champion, National Field Champion or National Amateur Field Champion. These are abbreviated as follows:

> Field Champion — FC or FLD CH
> Amateur Field Champion — AFC or AFLD CH
> National Field Champion — NFC of NFLD CH
> National Amateur Field Champion — NAFC
> OF NAFLD CH

Notice that all of these titles contain the word "Field." This means that they won the title in the field under the arduous testing of field trials. These retriever field trials are won by dogs who are vastly superior in retrieving desire, love of water, courage, intelligence, and trainability. Field trials are the ultimate test for the working retriever, testing fully all the traits desirable for the superior duck-hunting dog.

For your hunting purposes, it's best to avoid selecting a pup from a litter whose pedigree is packed with ancestors bearing the title of simply "Champion," abbreviated "CH." This title, *without* the designation "Field" or "F," was won in the show ring for being judged according to breed

The schackled duck and the clipped wing pigeon. These will be important motivators for the inhibited, lethargic, submissive or unresponsive dog.

Behavior followed by reward builds our desired habits.

conformation standards as set forth by the AKC. These standards are concerned with appearance rather than performance, and without field trial background are hardly sufficient to make a good duck dog.

It's not a bad idea to seek the advice of a field trial enthusiast or professional trainer in picking your litter. He will probably have knowledge of many of the past and present stars of the field trial circuit. One facet of advice that is important to you is that of trainability. How easy was "FC Fido" to train? This is a fairly critical factor since you plan to train one of Fido's pups. Why not try to make your job easier? Look for superior ancestors who were also easy to train. Another hint of trainability lies in the title "AFC Fido." The "AFC" indicates that "AFC Fido" excelled in the Amateur All-Age Stake, meaning that he was handled by an amateur, as opposed to a professional trainer. If you ask around and discover that he was also trained by an amateur then you have a stronger indicator of trainability.

If you think that all this selection and superior breeding is expensive, then you're right. However, the purchase price is the cheapest part of a puppy. If you add all of the time you're going to put into training pup, and all the years you're going to spend hunting with him, the result makes a couple of hundred dollars price difference seem rather inconsequential.

Merely being registered is definitely not a guarantee of the ideal retriever. Far fom it. There are many registered retrievers running around who are low on brain power and horse power. So go for the superior breeding where the ancestors have proven themselves. Even this is no guarantee, but the odds will be vastly increased.

After you have picked the litter, you come to the easiest part, picking the individual puppy. Pick the pup who appeals to you the most. This methods seems to be as successful as any other. The problem with puppy-picking is puppies. Bear in mind that puppies change greatly in appearance and behavioral characteristics between the ages of 6 weeks and 12 months. The way they are raised has a large influence on what behavioral characteristics they will demonstrate at 12 months of age. So just grab one and raise him properly.

Raising The Puppy — That young puppy you've picked is smart enough to train himself if you don't interfere too much. Basically all you have to remember is that pup is a creature of habit and you are the determinant of the good or bad habits that he forms. You can exert a profound influence on pup during his first six months. You can, without any formal training program, develop that pup to the point where at six months of age he is ready to start formal training. At this point he is brave, breaks his neck to retrieve, and swims like a fish. He is tractable, likes to be around you, and is familiar with the basic commands "Here," "Sit," "Stay," and "No."

When I say familiar with basic commands, I mean pup recognizes them and responds *when he feels like responding.* What I call formal training will develop him to the point where he will respond positively and consistently. Also the six month age figure should have some latitude. Six months

Squat down and clap and encourage to get pup to come.

13

Tennis balls are great fun to retrieve.

is about right for the average pup, but unfortunately pups are not all average. Therefore, it may be five months for some, or eight or nine months for others. It will vary with pup's personality (which will be discussed in Chapter 4), but we can say that, at some point, pup's genetics plus your puppy raising program will result in a pup who's ready to start formal training. In most cases, the raising is probably as important as the genetics.

I think the single most important factor in raising a puppy is that he be raised in the house. He needs lots of love and affection, lots of playing with the kids, and lots of exposure to strange sights and sounds. He'll get all of this in the house. The love, affection and play go towards developing a bond between you and pup such that he cares whether you're pleased with him or angry with him. It makes that pat on the head worth a lot and gives you a valuable reward for use in later training. Conversely, the pup who's raised in the kennel with a minimum of human contact will be harder to train. Reward will be less effective with him. He doesn't relate as well to you and doesn't care as much about that pat on the head. You'll have to use more force to train him. Further down the scale, the pup raised in the kennel with nearly no human contact will be shy, spooky, neurotic, and probably, for all practical purposes, untrainable.

Raising pup in the house may bring forth visions of stained rugs and odors, but this is easy to circumvent. Give him a puppy crate. Whenever he is unsupervised, put him in the crate. Very few puppies will soil their own nest. Of course, he should be let out on a consistent schedule and taken directly outside. I say consistent because pup must learn to predict the schedule and be able to pace himself accordingly. When he is very young, every two hours in the day time is optimal. This can be stretched with age. To help him make it through the night, don't give him any food or water for three hours prior to bedtime. Take him out before you turn in and again first thing in the morning. Be consistent and that first urination or defecation in the house should never occur. After a few weeks, presto! He's going to the door to ask to be let out, and you've formed a good habit. Pup has house broken himself and has been spared the neurosis brought on by twenty foot giants screaming at him, rubbing his nose in puppy mess, and throwing him out the door.

Here are the main points on puppy training, starting at six weeks of age.

Walks in woods and field are great for pup.

Expose pup to a variety of terrain and cover.

Introduce him to a dead pigeon. Tease him a bit with it first.

Coming when called is of paramount importance. Retrievers are born wanting to retrieve but not necessarily wanting to come to you. This must be reinforced. Remember that you are twenty feet tall to that puppy and very imposing. So every time you call him, squat down low, clap your hands, and call him playfully. When he gets to you, pet and praise him lavishly. If you do this consistently, he'll consistently come to you. By the time he is six months old he will hopefully be such a prisoner of habit that he won't be able to not come to you when called. The other magic trick is moving away from pup. Nearly all young puppies have a tendency to follow, so if pup isn't coming to you, move away from him. If you move far enough away and pup sees that you're leaving, then he'll come to you. He doesn't want to be left there alone. When he gets to you, pet and praise him lavishly. Whenever pup comes to you he should be so rewarded. This is an example of using some common sense and a little knowledge of puppy responses to produce a desired response. Repetition of this will build a habit.

If it's too late for the easy way and pup has already learned to play tag with you, then the solution lies in a checkcord. This is a 10 or 15 foot length of ¼ inch polypropylene rope (ski rope). This rope is lightweight and floats. Attach it to the plain leather collar with D ring which pup has been wearing for a few days. Just take pup for walks wearing the checkcord for the first few sessions. Periodically, when pup's attention is elsewhere, step on the rope, call him to you, and then gently reel him in. When he arrives, pet and praise lavishly. Don't introduce any retrieving until he's feeling comfortable with the rope. We don't want any bad associations with retrieving. Do not lose your patience and abuse him. He is just a puppy and the "pull and praise" method will work if you stick with it.

Meanwhile, we've hopefully started pup's retrieving program, using a dummy or stuffed sock.

The main points here are:
1. Don't let pup start the "tag game."
2. Success in each exercise.
3. Don't overdo it. Keep the lessons short.

The big trick on the first and subsequent retrieves is not to grab the dummy, sock or whatever, from the pup as he returns with it. Just reach for the pup gently, then pet and praise him lavishly for a moment or two, and then take the dummy. Grabbing at the dummy as pup arrives can frequently start him jumping away and progress to a full-fledged game of tag or tug-of-war. This game is sometimes referred to as "keep-away," "Catch me if you can," and several other less polite descriptions. This behavior of chase and be chased seems to be instinctive and is fairly common in pups while playing with each other. What you as the trainer want to do is use this behavior as a training device. When pup's not coming to you, dart away from him to trigger his response of chasing you. Conversely, when he is coming to you with the dummy, don't lunge at him and trigger his desire to be chased.

If squatting, clapping and encouragement don't work, run away from him to get him to bring it back to you.

The main reason people grab at the dummy as pup returns is that they are worried about him dropping it. However, this works in reverse since the lunging and grabbing will frequently startle pup into dropping it. The next phase will be the tag!

The proper solution to dropping dummies lies first in giving pup something that fits comfortably in his mouth and is fun to carry. For the very small pup, a pair of rolled up socks is great. As he grows you can progress to a small canvas dummy. Secondly, as mentioned previously, pet and praise pup when he arrives with the dummy. *You are rewarding him* for having the dummy in his mouth *while he has it in his mouth.* Then gently take it. If he holds on, simply pry open his mouth with your fingers and take it. Never pull the dummy from his mouth as this can start a game of tug-of-war and progress to tag. If you are doing all the above and he's still dropping it, don't worry about it. The conditioned retrieve portion of the formal training program will take care of it.

The exception to the rule of never playing tug-of-war is the puppy who is not interested in retrieving. Then you use tag, tug-of-war, and anything else you can think of to break loose that retrieving instinct and help him develop the desire to have that dummy in his mouth. A small rubber ball will sometimes work wonders here.

If you have a pup that has learned to run off to the bushes with the dummy, then resort to the rope and "Pull and Praise" routine. One important point about the rope is that you do not want pup to become educated as to when it

If you are 6 foot-two, then it's even more important to get down low to attract pup to you.

Don't lunge at pup.

Reach for pup, not the bird.

Pet him awhile before taking the bird.

is on and when it is not. Therefore, when you start using the rope, have it on *every* time you work pup until he's consistently coming to you, and then leave it on for another month.

The next point to remember on retrieving is to insure that pup enjoys success on every retrieve. You want him to *always find the dummy where he saw it fall and find it quickly.* This will further and continue his enthusiasm and confidence. Therefore, keep the retrieving easy and on short grass or in the water. When pup has to spend fifteen minutes fighting heavy brush on a hot day to find a dummy, his enthusiasm will diminish.

With an eight week old pup, you should start out with six foot retrieves and gradually increase the distance on a daily basis, proportionately with pup's confidence and proficiency. Don't give pup more than four or five retrieves a day. He's young, has a short attention span, and is easily tired. Ten or twenty retrieves in a row will tend to tire him and he may start losing retrieving desire or he may decide tag is more fun. These puppies are born wanting to retrieve but they can be trained to quit. This is usually accomplished by overworking the young puppy, similar to kids and candy. Small doses make them want it that much more, but a few good overdoses can make them swear off it for quite a while.

There are several things a puppy should be introduced to at a young age. An eight week old pup will swim like a fish when introduced to the water properly. Conversely, it can sometimes take weeks to teach swimming to a year old pup who has never been in the water. A good way to introduce a pup to water is either to wade in yourself and entice him to follow or let him follow an older dog. One important point on the water introduction: don't do it in the winter in cold water and *never throw him in.* You want all pup's associations with the water to be happy and fun.

Another introduction that should occur at a young age is to birds. Toss a dead pigeon for pup. He'll do one of three things: (1) He'll pick it up and bring it back while you squat and clap your hands, in which case you pet and praise first and then gently take the bird. If he has a death grip, then just push his gum against a tooth and take it while petting him. We want no bad associations with birds. (2) He'll pounce on the bird, drag it off to the bushes, and commence eating it. In this case do nothing. Let him finish or tire of it, whichever comes first. People generally over-react to a puppy eating a bird, but it's not that big a problem. Often it will correct itself by simply putting pup on dummies for a month or two. The more persistant pups can be cured when they are older by putting them through a simple conditioned retrieve regimen. It is a normal course of action to get a bird-shy or a reluctant retriever to eat birds in order to trigger his retrieving instinct. It is much easier to teach a dog *not* to eat birds than it is to teach him to like birds or to like retrieving. (3) He may be afraid of the bird in which case we tease him with it, try to get him to play tug-of-war with the bird, etc. If this doesn't work, then leave the bird in the crate with the pup for a couple of hours and see if he'll get hungry. Remember, this is a dead pigeon, not a big flapping live one which would probably scare any small puppy on first contact.

When pup is 4 or 5 months old and doing 20 or 30 yard retrieves you can introduce him to the gun. Put a friend out in the field about 20 or 30 yards to throw the bird. If pup is a bird-eater then dummies will do nicely. Give pup a couple of retrieves with your friend throwing the dummy or bird. This should get pup properly motivated. Then have your friend shoot a .22 blank as he throws. Continue punctuating the retrieves with gunfire for the next several sessions and progress to the shotgun. Pup will associate gunfire with the activity he loves most — retrieving.

Gunshyness is not something that pup is born with. It is usually man made and I can suggest one excellent method for doing this. In order to find out if a young puppy is gunshy, walk up to him and shoot a shotgun. He will probably be gunshy. His reaction will be very similar to what yours would be if someone walked behind you and triggered a volley of twelve gauge magnums without warning.

Your friend and dummy thrower in the field has another function besides introducing the gun. He can provide distance on retrieves. As stated earlier, pup is a creature of habit. If you do all the throwing, he's going to get in the habit of hunting at the distance you can throw. Everything he's retrieved has been found at that distance, so that's where he expects to find it. Therefore you want to stretch out those retrieves occasionally with a helper. Don't, however, stretch him out too rapidly — we want him to be successful most of the time. One of the best ways to do this is to leave your helper in one place while you and pup back up progressively on each retrieve to increase the distance. Pup will be successful because he will be finding the dummy in the same place every time, yet you will be increasing the distance.

This is the correct way to call a puppy.

A pleasant diversion and also a most important factor in pup's training before he's six months old involves exposure to different surroundings. Take him whenever possible on walks in the woods and fields with pup running loose. This will bring out his hunting instincts, make him bolder, and reinforce the bond with his master. Along the same lines of developing free spirit, one should not subject pup to rigid obedience training or drills until he's had some of the activities previously mentioned and not before he's six months old. He's got to have time in his life to play and develop emotionally. A wild, brave youngster of six months is a much better candidate for more formal training than a shy, inhibited, and neurotic pup.

All the obedience for the young pup should be taught as a game. The main lessons are come and sit. There is really no necessity for a young puppy to heel. If you're good to him and pet him when he comes, he'll want to be around you anyway. You will also find that a bond will form with the retrieving. Pup will stick around just in case you might throw him a dummy. I feel that demanding a young pup to heel or stay too rigidly is overly inhibiting. Save those lessons until he's over six months. However there is no harm done if you can get him to sit progressively for longer periods of time for his supper, or similar game type teaching.

He should learn the command "no," preferably in the house, and especially when he's chewing on your oriental rug or a lamp cord. Tell him "NO." If you get no response tap him on the snout and a few repetitions should teach him the command.

The ultimate goal at the end of six months should be a wild retrieving fool outdoors who has a somewhat civilized nature in the house. Don't forget that all associations with birds, water, and retrieving should be fun and successful. You are forming good habits, avoiding the bad ones, and dealing with a very young animal. Be patient and don't overreact.

"The Old Man", Rocky
FC-AFC IRON WOOD'S ROCKY
12 Yr. Old Yellow

21

Chapter 3
Relating to your Pup

Our training program is going to transform pup into a well-mannered hunting companion who is a pleasure to have along on a day's hunt. He'll walk quietly at heel without continuous badgering.

He'll sit when and where he's told and stay there until released. He will sit quietly while you're calling ducks and also while you're shooting. He'll retrieve vigorously on command and deliver birds tenderly to hand. He will take a line on blind retrieves where he hasn't seen the bird fall, and also stop on a whistle command and take hand signals to direct him to the bird. In short, he'll be under control and a pleasant hunting companion.

We're going to achieve this through a structured training program which will take 4 to 6 months. It will cost you an average of 15 to 20 minutes per day of your time, and a good portion of it can be done in the backyard and garage.

The training program should be viewed from two angles. We want to nurture and develop pup's natural instinct to retrieve while gradually imposing more control on him. We'd like to keep him hot on retrieving while gradually increasing control. We'll do this by a progressive series of control drills which will develop habits, and subsequently merge with the retrieving behavior.

Habit formation is the way we'll train pup. This is the way pup learns to respond consistently to commands. Notice the word "consistently." We can teach pup to sit on command in one lesson, but he's not going to sit every time you give the command. He'll know that the command means for him to sit, but he's not going to respond consistently. The least distraction will cause him to ignore the command. The habit of consistent response is what we'll develop through drill and repetition. A dog is a creature of habit, and with enough repetition, he can be conditioned to the point of being unable to disobey.

yellow lab with cock pheasant—

Starting a 4-month old puppy in the water, the first toss should be quite short.

Conversely, too much repetition will inhibit pup and may dampen his retrieving desire, so we must maintain a balance. Also, we'll keep the training sessions short and pleasant for pup so that he enjoys them.

Another aspect of the training program is communicating with pup. Obviously if you're going to train pup, then you must be able to communicate with him. Let's go back and look again at his wolf ancestors. The wolf pecking order in the pack tells us that the individual wolf feels more secure when he know what his place is in the pack. The same is true of dogs relative to their "pack" which consists of you and the family. Dogs are more comfortable when they know what is expected of them. This attitude forms the foundation for our first training rule: *Be consistent.* By *consistent,* I mean maintain your dominance relative to pup. Don't spoil him five days a week and then expect him to obey *at all times* on the weekend. If you want him obedient and responsive on hunts and training sessions then demand it all the time. On the other hand, you don't want to be extremist to the point of non-stop nagging. Don't expect consistent compliance with commands before he's well trained. What you want is a basic underlying understanding between you and pup — *only you* are the boss. This is not to say that you should be drilling him all the time. Pup should have times of play and times of companionship, understanding the difference between work and play. Maintaining your dominance will not make pup like you less. To the contrary, respect will provide an added dimension to his devotion to you, his master and pal.

The best rule I've found is not to give a command unless I'm in the mood and in a position to enforce it. If partially-

The second toss a bit further.

And the third a little further. We're trying to build confidence with success.

trained pup is on the other side of the lake and hot on the trail of a rabbit, I'm not going to call him because I'm fairly sure he won't obey. Giving pup a command in such a situation or circumstance is actually non-productive and, in fact, training him to disobey. Similarly, try not to put pup in a situation where he must be corrected. Consistent response is developed through drill and repetition rather than testing and correcting him frequently which tends to cause his dislike of training. Your objective is to gradually introduce distractions as the habits become stronger. In other words, after three or four days of heeling drill, don't walk pup into a crowd of people and expect him to heel. He's not going to do it. After three or four weeks of proper drill, however, you can walk him into Grand Central Station on a leash and expect him to heel with a minimum of correction.

This dog training process is a combination of conditioning and bluff. One of our main tools will be a rope. We start pup at the end of a rope so that he's always under control and we can insure response to a command. This is developed by drill and repetition into habit. At the same time, never give pup a command when you don't have control. When he's one hundred yards away, wearing a 20 foot rope, and finds some terrific scent to follow, don't call him to come. You don't want him to learn that the rope is only 20 feet long. We'll make the habits strong enough in the training program so that we can eventually discard the rope. While the training is in progress, however, we don't want pup to learn too much about ropes. We don't want him to learn that he must obey only when he's wearing a rope, and we don't want him to learn the length of the rope. You want to bluff and condition pup into thinking that the rope is always present and infinitely long.

Yellow Lab ~
5 Yr. Old

There will be a strong temptation to show off your pup's progress in training after a few weeks. Resist that temptation. If you take off the rope before the habits are strong enough, pup is going to find out that you don't have control of him when he's not wearing the rope. He will learn to obey *only* when a rope is on but *not* when it is off. This diminishes the rope's value as a training tool and needlessly increases the length of time required for your training program.

For you, the trainer, a major problem will be that of recognizing when pup is disobeying as opposed to when he is confused. The solution is to always give the pup the benefit of the doubt. *Assume he's confused,* analyze the problem, and simplify it, or come back to it after some remedial training. For example, let's say that you're having a problem with pup on his water retrieves. On his return he's stopping just off the bank and playing with the bird. The problem here is not the playing but the failure to respond to the command "here." He will not stop to play if he's responding well to the command "here." The solution lies in going back to yard work and obedience drills until his "here" response is reinforced sufficiently. Then go back to the water work.

Another example commonly seen is breaking, i.e. taking off to retrieve a fallen bird before he's commanded to do so. Here we have a deficiency of response to the command "sit" or "stay." The solution lies again in more yard work and drill with emphasis on sitting and staying.

Essentially, we're preparing a pup whose control habits have been sufficiently developed to minimize correction on retrieves in the field. Don't continuously correct pup in the field, for it will be associated with retrieving. This will dull his retrieving desire and slow him down.

As a further aid to minimizing corrections in the field, we'll do as much as possible of the early retrieving work with dummies instead of birds. Dummies are much less of a distraction than birds and will allow us to build and strengthen control while pup is retrieving. He'll be much less tempted to disobey as the habits of obedience, steadiness, and delivering to hand become more firmly established. Then, and only then, should we progress to birds.

Notice that I mention *dummies as much as possible.* Birds are going to be our prime motivator for those dogs who are lethargic or inhibited. Also a lot of birds will help with the dog who tends to be unresponsive to people. He'll associate you with the birds and begin to respond.

Trainer Behavior

Many problems encountered by beginning trainers are people problems, not dog problems. A major factor is consistency. For pup to be comfortable, motivated, and a good student, he must know what to expect from you, his trainer. With the consistent trainer, he *always* knows. This is the trainer who understands his objectives and has a well-planned and scheduled program as presented in this book. All you add is a little work and some insight into your dog's personality.

One of the major threats to consistency is the dog expert. There is an abundance of dog experts, and they generally know one magic method or another which is going to miraculously transform your dog. It doesn't quite work that way. Listen to them and make notes if you must, but don't immediately try their methods. File them away and at the proper time, compare them with your planned scheduled program. If they are compatible, implement them in a planned, scheduled, and logical manner. The trainer who trains by the "short cut" or quick solution method is going to produce an anxious, neurotic pup who is continuously worrying about what the next trick is going to be.

Another threat to pup's emotional stability stems from our unwillingness to separate work from play. Pup needs play and companionship, but he also needs discipline. Rest assured, he's quite capable of recognizing the difference. Some people are not so inclined. For the best results and a happy pup, insist upon discipline during work and training, but not during play.

As an example, if you're engaged in a frenzied game of frisbee with pup, don't suddenly throw a command at him.

Nesting Hen
Wood Duck

Why some do this eludes me. If it's for the purpose of assessing the dog's training, it is an unfair practice. Pup responds to circumstances as well as commands and a play session doesn't trigger pup's mind towards obeying. So, for pup's sake, keep the work and play separate.

This is not to say that play cannot be used to some extent in training — it should, *but only as a reward — not as a testing device.* Reward play is particularly important in young puppies under six months of age, when virtually all training should be reward oriented — the reward being play or food.

Our objective is to train pup as a one-command retriever. Put another way, we require an immediate response to a singular command spoken in a normal tone of voice. To accomplish this we must, in general, train in this same required manner. There will be times in the training process when repeating commands will be necessary to establish some desired behavior, but avoid the habit of repeating commands. Remember the "one command" objective. Check your own performance occasionally. It's easy for people to get into the habit of repeating commands. This is basically the result of one being lazy and not wanting to go back and perform the remedial drills on areas where pup is regressing. When you find yourself slipping into the pattern of repeating commands, recognize it and go back to remedial drills immediately. Don't fall into the next trap which is shouting. The only time for shouting in a dog training or handling program is when pup is so far afield that it's necessary for him to hear you. Shouting is not inherently meaningful to pup. It usually has an acquired or learned meaning because it's been followed occasionally by a loss of temper and punishment on the part of a trainer. A normally spoken command can acquire the same meaning in the same manner. It is, however, vastly preferable that the meaning be learned by drill and conditioning rather than acquired by lost temper and punishment.

Loud noise is not a dire threat to pup. It generally will either excite him or scare him. If it frightens him, he may have acquired that reaction from your lost temper and his consequent punishment. Or he may be the type of young pup who has been isolated in the kennel for long periods of time and is frightened of any loud noise due to lack of exposure. In any event, neither state, of being frightened or excited, is conducive to improving command response or healthy learning.

The dire threat should only be used on pup when he is testing you on proven behavior that *you know that he knows.* When he's testing your limits, stand on your tiptoes, raise your hackles, and project that command from deep in your chest in a low rumble. That is a threat to pup that he truly understands. But, don't abuse it. Don't slip into the habit of always threatening or pup will respond only to the threatening command and not to the normally spoken one. If you find yourself threatening frequently, then go back and re-establish the responses by drill and conditioning.

Johnny Marsh
hand-Made Reelfoot
Lake Caller—

Pup either doesn't know how or won't jump in truck. What do you do?

Try the easy way first.

"Pup, kennel." Repetition will bring about the desired response.

Shouting and repeating commands both fall under the heading of nagging, and produce an unhappy, confused, and worried pup. Nagging is usually a trainer reaction to poor command response from pup. When pup fails to respond to a single normally articulated command, it's not because he didn't hear you. He either isn't well conditioned or doesn't feel like complying. In either case the solution doesn't lie in repeating or shouting. The proper reaction is to analyze. Has pup had enough drill and conditioning to be properly responsive? If not, then back up and do something about it. If the root of the problem is a dominant, hyperactive or insensitive personality then the solution is in correction. Don't nag continuously to keep pup from making a mistake. Let him make it and then correct him for it. He expects correction when he's checking your limits. It's his nature. He'll accept correction, accept that the limits are still there, and respect you for it. Work will go on. It's the nagging that wears him down.

Another training problem lies in the attitude you project toward pup during training. If you, the trainer, are unsure of what you want from pup and hesistant in your *requests,* then pup is going to tend to give confused, hesitant responses. Conversely, as a confident handler who is clear and decisive in your *demands,* you will elicit sharp, positive responses from pup. What I'm saying is, act decisively whether you feel that way or not. It is much better to give the wrong command or do the wrong thing decisively than to

Crowe (?)
Drake Woodduck
1 9 8 3

fumble around wondering whether it is right or wrong. Pup's going to tend to reflect your emotional state so at least act like you know what you're going to do in each training session.

This brings us to a discussion of that nemesis of the dog trainer: the lost temper. The best way to handle it when you feel it coming on is to put pup in the kennel. Come back and try that lesson tomorrow. On those days when you're operating on a short fuse, don't take pup out of the kennel. A lost temper and consequent horror show sends the training program straight backwards. Depending on your pup's temperament, one blow-up can create a problem that may take days, weeks, or even months to repair. Thus, there are times when leaving pup in the kennel will speed up the training program. A sensible alternative on short fuse days is to put pup in the car, find a big area of woods or fields, and have a companionable walk with no control required of either of you. It'll improve the outlook for you and your pup.

The temper act is usually a result of impatience with pup's progress — expecting too much too soon. You've got to remember that you're dealing with an animal who learns by habit formation. He doesn't learn by sudden inspiration, demonstration, or force. The habits are formed by repetition and this takes time and drill. Frequently the results of today's training won't appear until next week when the habits become strong enough to start showing some consistant response. Along these same lines, don't confuse age with training experience. Suppose pup is 2 years old with very little training and is being upstaged by the one-year-old pup next door whose more conscientious owner has been working at it for the last six months. Your neighbor's pup isn't better; he's just had more training. Expecting your two year old sparsely-trained retriever to perform better because of his age is as absurd as expecting him to be trained by sleeping with this book under his pillow.

Don't, however, go out and try to cram six months of training into one catch-up. Most dogs will only become confused and you may end up driving out the retrieving desire.

Remember, keep your training sessions short, sweet, and consistent. Do this, while avoiding trainer's traps, and you'll end up with a well-trained, eager and stylish retriever.

Chapter 4
When to Start Training Pup

When we talk about **when** to start training your pup, the first item discussed would be the definition of training. Let's divide it into 2 categories: natural behavior and control. The highest priority goes to pup's natural behavior. This is pup's retrieving desire and hunting behavior which should be well developed before superimposing the control.

The importance of developing this retrieving desire can't be overstated. This is what makes pup keep going back into that cold water again and again to retrieve your ducks. It is what makes him fight that heavy cover for a half hour or more, and finally root out that cripple. This is something you can't make pup do. Its an instinct that needs to be nurtured and developed.

Conversely, a strict diet of this will result in an uncontrollable, wild streak. So at some point we want to start superimposing control.

The control training is going to inhibit pup's natural behavior a bit. Therefore, you want to start when the natural behavior is very high and well established, and you want to superimpose the control gradually.

The subject of bringing along a 6 week old puppy to the point of beginning control training has already been covered in Chapter 2, but how about the older dog you want to start training?

Bring him along the same way you would the puppy but with an abbreviated program. He's probably been socialized and had lots of love and affection, etc. The main thing we need to do with him now is develop the hunting and retrieving instincts. Do this the same way described in the Puppy Raising Chapter.

When you are starting with an older dog, you may encounter a few problems. The most prevalent one that I see is the dog who has been taught to run away. How are you going to develop the retrieving behavior in dog if every time you throw something for him, he grabs it and runs off?

Very simple. Tie a long rope to his collar and hold the other end in your hand. Then throw the dummy for the dog to retrieve and bring him back with the rope. Keep the rope on the dog and in your hand until you are absolutely sure he is not going to revert. This could be as long as several weeks or after you finish the conditioned retrieve training. It will vary greatly from dog to dog.

A variation of this is to put a 10 foot rope on the dog and give him his retrieves in the water. Be sure you can get a hand or foot on the rope as he comes out of the water.

Another problem that can be encountered in older dogs who've missed the proper development is a dormant retrieving instinct. This is the dog that shows no interest in retrieving.

You'd like pup retrieving eagerly in the water before you start the control training.

When I say he shows no interest in retrieving, I assume that you've given a good effort to getting him interested. You've tried a lot of play with all sorts of objects like balls, sticks, gloves, and frizbees, as well as socks and towels, etc., and have tried the retrieving in the water. I also assume you've tried it with pigeons, both dead and wing-clipped. If you've given this a good honest effort and still get no response then you've got a disinterested retriever.

Here are three courses of action:

1. Get the dog started by letting him eat birds. If you can get him wanting that bird badly enough, then you can get him to run out and grab a bird that you throw. You'll probably have to haul him back to you with the rope but you'll have that basic pattern of retrieving behavior started.

If he doesn't like to bring it back, a long checkcord eliminates escape routes.

Here's how to begin: Put your dog in his kennel and leave him there. Don't feed him the first day. (Of course he should have water at all times.) The second day, put a freshly killed pigeon in with him. If he eats it then feed him as usual, leaving him in the kennel. Feed him another pigeon the second and third days and feed him his usual meals. The fourth day, put a live clipped-wing pigeon in with him and let him kill it. The next day do the same. Now you're ready to try a few short retrieves. Take your dog out on a long rope and try a few short retrieves with frozen pigeons. (He can't eat those.) Each time he brings back a bird, whether pulled in by rope or voluntarily, pet and praise him before prying the bird out of his mouth. Don't harrass him about being hardmouthed. Our main concern is the retrieving. We'll take care of the hard mouth later with the conditioned retrieve training.

If the frozen birds didn't work, then give him a few days of short retrieves on the rope with freshly killed or live clipped-wing pigeons. Again, when he gets back with the bird, probably as a result of your pulling him back by rope, then pry what's left of the bird out of his mouth and pet and praise. Then try again the transition to frozen birds.

After you've had your dog retrieving frozen birds (only 3 or 4 retrieves per day) for a week or so, then try a dummy with a pigeon wing taped to it. Use this for a week or so and then try just the dummy. Sometimes this transition will work and sometimes not. If it doesn't, just stick with the frozen birds to develop his retrieving instinct for a few weeks prior to starting obedience training. When you're going through the obedience program, use frozen birds instead of dummies for the required retrieves. We'll transfer to dummies later in the conditioned retrieve training.

2. The second course of action with your non-retriever, especially if you didn't feed him for a couple of days and still couldn't get him to respond, is a recommendation that you give up and get another pup.

3. If you're determined to continue and keep trying, there is one further course of action. You can go ahead with the obedience training, eliminating

A foot on the checkcord works wonders toward improving the direction of his return.

the retrieving portion, and take him through the conditioned retrieve training. The odds here on turning out an aggressive retriever are poor. I would guess that one out of three will turn out good, but if you're determined, go ahead.

The last case I'll cover is the dog who shows interest in retrieving but doesn't pick up the object. When you throw something he runs out after it but won't pick it up. This trait also makes it somewhat difficult to develop the retrieving behavior so you'll need to change it.

Basically, the solution here is to try the same things as with the dog with no interest in retrieving. Try a lot of play and throw short retrieves with different objects on land and in the water, looking for that something which he will pick up. Try tug-of-war with something and then throw it. He'll usually pick it up, and you'll have that to develop the retrieving behavior. Then you can gradually transfer to other objects like training dummies.

In the unlikely event that the above doesn't work then put him through obedience without the prescribed retrieves. Cut the obedience program in half because it will be more of a grind for the dog without the retrieves. Then take him through the conditioned retrieve training. The odds for the dog who charges out on a retrieve but doesn't pick it up are excellent. The conditioned retrieve will cure most dogs and give you a good eager retriever. To maximize the odds, you should try the earlier methods to get a good retrieving behavior base prior to the obedience and conditioned retrieve training.

In closing, let me remind you of the value of long walks in the woods and fields. These are quite valuable in bringing out the hunting and exploration behavior in pups as well as older dogs.

callin' in
the Labs—
Self-Portrait
Crowe 1982

Chapter 5
OBEDIENCE

Before starting obedience, let's take an advanced look at the finished product so we know what we're aiming for. This is the dog who heels, sits, stays and comes on command consistently, *anytime, anywhere*. He responds to command without shouting and without repeating commands. We're going to achieve this in 4 to 6 weeks for the average dog.

This basic obedience course is not going to make pup steady nor is it going to make him deliver to hand or respond to hand signals. It does form the basis for his further training which will eventually result in the completely trained retriever. Just as the student must master basic arithmetic before tackling geometry, so must pup master basic obedience before advancing to subsequent demands of the training program.

The obedience program is quite important in that it's going to set the tone and influence pup's attitude toward all of his subsequent training. Therefore, we want pup to enjoy it as much as possible. I say "as much as possible" because of the wide spectrum of personalities in the dog population. Some dogs will like it and some of them will not. There are several things you can do to influence pup to enjoy obedience as much as possible. This is most important since the pup is not only learning obedience, but is learning *how* to learn. The tone we set at this point can greatly influence all of pup's future training.

To begin with, confine pup for a couple of hours prior to each training session. Then his attitude is "Oh boy, here comes the boss. I can get out and go to work now." This is much preferable to "Oh damn, I'm having such a good time playing with the kids, and here comes that turkey to haul me away and drag me around on a rope for 30 minutes."

Another aspect of this attitude adjustment comes with throwing pup a couple of dummies before starting each session and a couple at the end of each session. You want pup coming out of the kennel with happy expectations and going back into the kennel happy.

The lessons are geared to a duration of about 10 minutes. The frequency of sessions should be about one per day for the first four or five lessons and then at your option you can increase them to two or even three lessons a day if you wish. The brevity of the lessons is designed to keep them from becoming too boring to pup. We don't want it to become a grind.

We initially limit ourselves to one lesson per day because pup is entering a new environment, i.e. a controlled environment which is going to induce in him a certain amount of stress. The one-lesson-per-day rule is an effort to minimize that stress. As pup becomes more comfortable in the training environment and more proficient at performing the desired behavior, you can build up to two or three lessons per day.

One method of confining pup prior to his lesson. He doesn't learn anything by watching, but the restraint does tend to influence him to like the work more.

Happy dummies before each obedience lesson. Accompany them with the breaking signal, "HUP, HUP, HUP. . ."

The training equipment.

If you do go to two or three lessons a day, you should follow what I call the four hour rule. I don't like to put pup through two training sessions any closer together than four hours. For some unknown reason this seems to be a minimum time for the first lesson to be absorbed into pup's brain.

Another practice you can use to influence pup to like training is to deprive him of all other activities for the first few weeks of the training program. Confine him to the kennel except for his training lessons. Then he has no basis for comparison to judge training as being less enjoyable.

This may seem to be a bit harsh on pup, but taken in perspective it is kinder to him. A few weeks of confinement now will improve his attitude toward all the rest of his subsequent training. Additionally he won't be indulging in behaviors that may counteract his training, thus making the training easier on him. If he spends two hours a day playing tag with the kids, how long do you think it will take you, at 10 minutes a day, to obtain a consistent "HERE" response?

One unfortunate practice which seems to be quite widespread is that of letting pup run around a bit upon exiting the kennel, before starting the training session. This is supposed to let pup burn off some energy and thus be easier to handle during the subsequent training session. It does both of these. It also trains pup to be easy to handle when he feels like it, instead of when you feel like it. Additionally, it *trains* pup through repetition that those first 10 or 15 minutes after coming out of the kennel *belong* to pup; *he can do as he pleases* during that time. This is hardly consistent with training for a 100% response from pup.

Along the same vein I frequently wonder, upon hearing of another good retriever's death under automobile wheels, whether it occurred during those first 10 to 15 minutes after coming out of the car or kennel; a death resulting from trained disobedience. Hence you will see that most of the lessons begin with the statement "Take pup from the kennel under control." For those lessons that don't begin with that statement, it should be assumed.

Before starting the obedience training you should be familiar with the training equipment. This will consist of a 10 ft. piece of 1/4 inch polypropylene rope (ski rope), a stick or switch and a pinch collar. The pinch collar is also termed the J.A.S.A. training collar. It is a leather slip collar with brass tacks (dull them slightly with a file) protruding from the inner surface. This collar looks quite formidable, but it is actually a much more humane training device than is the chain choke collar. The chain collar requires a certain amount of skill and timing to be effective. Even in skillful hands the chain collar may cause physical damage to the throats of dominant aggressive dogs. The pinch collar is a different story. It is constructed of stiff leather, such that when pup pulls against it, the collar tightens, pinching his neck. When he quits pulling, the collar spreads itself open relieving the pinch. The collar, rather than your hands,

Always hold pup when putting on the pinch collar. You don't want him ever to succeed at not accepting it.

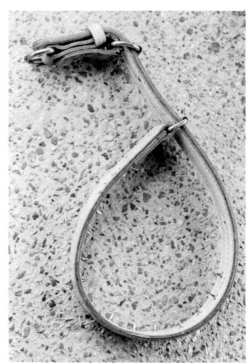

The JASA training collar, also termed "pinch collar." Dull the spikes a bit with a file.

The pinch collar properly placed with roller to the outside. This placement is correct for the tougher dog. For the more sensitive pup put it below the regular collar.

Beginning the heeling lessons.

Hugging your leg is unacceptable. Bump pup with your knee till he stops hugging.

Pup is heeling properly. Note the amount of slack in rope. Also note that pup is watching handler in order to keep himself properly positioned.

provides the timing. A further advantage of the pinch collar is that pup chooses his own level of correction. When he is learning to heel, he will pull against the pinch collar to the degree that it becomes uncomfortable, then he'll back off. Pay attention to this; it'll tell you a lot about this particular pup's sensitivity to correction. It'll help you determine the magnitude of force to use on pup during his training program. Some, being relatively sensitive to discomfort, require very little and some require a lot. This is a determination which must be made by the trainer for each individual dog.

Now, before we proceed to the first obedience lesson, let's check the prerequisites. Is pup's retrieving behavior firmly established? If not refer back to Chapter 4, "when to start training." Does pup give to his neck? By this I mean does he buck and fight when you put a regular leather collar and leash on him and try to lead him around? If he does, the first step in our step-by-step training program will be to take the fight out of his neck. To do this, we'll use an item that should be a permanent part of pup's wardrobe.

A good leather or nylon collar with sturdy "D" ring and identification plate attached will provide excellent insurance against loss of pup. At least, whoever finds him will know who he belongs to. Thus, there's hope that they will probably notify you. It is also much harder for pup to hang himself in the kennel when wearing the regular collar as opposed to the chain choke collar.

To teach pup to give to his neck, you put on his regular collar loose enough to get two fingers comfortably under it, but tight enough that he can't slip out of it. Then attach a rope or chain to the "D" ring of pup's regular collar and tie him to a stake or tree. If the weather is hot, make sure he is in the shade. He's going to fight that rope a bit and you don't want him to overheat.

Retire to the house and watch through the window. If it's hot and he's struggling to the extent of overheating, go out and calm him by speaking soothingly and giving him some water. If he's really getting hysterical, periodically go out and speak reassuringly to him. Don't release him as this would merely reward the struggling behavior and prolong the process. Remember, you're the good guy. You'd do something about this restraint if you could, but you can't. If you're not around, then pup is not going to associate all the bad feelings of this experience with you. He can blame the tree or the stake, but he can't blame you because you're not there. This surrender to the neck is also going to make the obedience training much easier and again avoid quite a bit of negative association with the trainer.

A couple of hours will result in surrender for most dogs. There are some, however, who might persist in fighting it for several days of hour sessions. You have to make that determination. The bottom line is the point when he has quit the fighting and struggling against the restraint. Then he's ready for obedience training.

LESSON 1

Take pup out of the kennel and attach your 10 foot rope to his regular leather collar. Throw him a couple of fun dummies. Incidentally, try not to use any commands when pup's engaged in the fun dummy retrieving. First, since he's not going to be in a frame of mind to obey, you'll be teaching him disobedience. Second, use of commands in this jazzing up tends initially to unjazz it for the pup. Also, on the fun dummies, give pup some happy verbal signal such as "hup, hup, hup" to tell him he can break. This will be consistent with our future requirement that pup not retrieve until commanded to do so. Hup...Hup...Hup will be the command *to break.*

After doing the two fun retrieves, unsnap your rope from the regular collar. Place the pinch collar on pup with the slip roller to the outside. Grasp the collar with your left hand at the point of attachment to the rope and lock your hand in such a position that pup's head will be about 6 inches off your left knee. If you want pup to heel on the right then use right hand and knee. Begin walking but don't give any commands. We don't want to use the command "heel" until lesson 4 or 5, when he's heeling properly. Thus the command will elicit and be associated with the desired behavior.

Pup can do any one of several things at this point. He can forge ahead; in which case he will pinch himself and after several tries, he will assume the correct position. He can lag back; in which case, keep walking while giving him verbal encouragement in the form of "good dog" or "atta boy." Or he can dig in and drag back. If this happens, you should stop, firmly tug him forward to the heel position, and then give him some slack so the pinch collar releases. Do this several times, then start walking again. The object with this lesson is to create a comfort zone for the heel position while every other position contains discomfort in the form of a pinch on the neck. One thing to keep in mind is that we want to end the session on a happy note, with pup getting a couple of "fun" retrieves.

So don't scare the retrieve out of him. While you're doing the heeling watch his ears and tail. If the ears go back and the tail curls up under his belly, you're doing too much pinching and not enough encouraging. Conversely if his tail is up and wagging and his head is cocked back, smiling over his shoulder at you as he drags you through the rose bushes, then obviously a little heavier hand is called for. If you've got the rare hardcase on whom the pinch collar seems to have no effect then shift the position of the collar. Put it up on his neck, just behind the ears. This is a tender spot. Your 60 year-old grandmother can control a Great Dane of equal weight when the pinch collar is so positioned.

Ten minutes is plenty for this session. Then give pup his two "fun" retrieves and "kennel" him.

Teaching pup to sit. Right hand pulls up and back on pinch collar while left hand pushes rump down.

Introduce pup to the stick in a pleasant manner.

Sitting with a pinch and tap.

Pup is learning to beat the tap.

LESSON 2

Take pup from the kennel under control on his rope. Give him the two fun retrieves. Put on the pinch collar and walk about for ten minutes with pup at heel. Then two "fun" retrieves and back to the kennel, under control (on rope).

LESSON 3

Take pup from kennel under control, with pinch collar and rope and give him his two "fun" retrieves. Heel as before for 2 or 3 minutes. He should be heeling with relatively little struggle. Now we'll add something. We're going to teach him to pay attention to the handler. Up to now you've been holding that pinch collar at its point of attachment to the rope and pup's been heeling in response to the pressure of the pinch collar anchored by your hand. Now we want to start programming him to heel by using his eyes rather than his sense of touch or sense of hearing. In this manner we'll end up with a pup that heels automatically, without continuous nagging from the handler. We're putting the responsibility for keeping himself at heel on pup's shoulders. More important, we'll end up with a pup who is programmed to pay attention to the handler. A pup who is looking at the handler is one who is paying attention, and one who is more prone to obey a command. This "sight" programming will carry over to pup's subsequent training and make it much easier.

To begin, shift your left hand off the pinch collar to a foot or two up the rope such that you have a belly of slack hanging down 6 inches or so off the ground. Start walking, keeping your eyes on pup. When he gets ahead of you or is otherwise distracted, quickly and sneakily turn 180 degrees and go the other way. This will result in a smart pinch on pup's neck. A few repetitions of this tactic should get pup to start using his eyes to keep himself at heel. If he starts leaning against your leg, then he's cheating. He's still trying to use his tactile sense for heeling. Bump against his shoulder with your knee until he stops the leaning. Eight or ten minutes of this is sufficient for lesson 3. Give him the fun retrieves and then to the kennel, under control.

LESSON 4

Take pup from the kennel under control. Throw him the happy dummies. Then heel him around for 3 to 5 minutes in the same manner as in the previous lesson. Next we'll teach "SIT."

Stop with pup at heel and grasp the pinch collar at point of attachment to rope, with your right hand. Command "SIT." Pull up and back steadily while pushing down on pup's rump with your left hand. As soon as pup's rump touches the ground, release the pressure of the collar and reward him with a few pats if appropriate. Do this 10 times. This should be sufficient to get pup sitting with just the pinch. If its not, then do it 10 more times with the pinch and push down on rump. If pup is not now sitting on just the pinch, then we need to get a bit more serious. Command

"SIT." Pull up on the pinch collar to the extent that pup's forepaws are clear of the ground. Hold him thus until that rump touches the ground. As soon as it does, release pressure and praise him and give a few pats.

When you've gotten 4 or 5 sits. with just the pinch, that's enough. Give him the two happy dummies and put him up.

LESSON 5

Take pup from the kennel under control and then give him two happy dummies. Heel him around for 3 to 5 minutes. Do 10 sits cued with light pinches. Then give him two happy dummies and put him up.

LESSON 6

Repeat lesson 5.

LESSON 7

Take pup from the kennel and give him the happy dummies. Heel him around for 2 or 3 minutes throwing in a few "sits" cued with light pinches.

Now we'll introduce the stick. Show it to pup. Let him sniff it. Brush it along his shoulders and body. Toss it for him to retrieve. We want pup to realize that the stick is not an inherently evil object. After this introduction, do a little heeling and then a "sit" with a light pinch and simultaneously a feather-light tap on the rump with the stick.

For those who are getting sloppy, let me inject a reminder on timing. The command "sit" should be immediately followed by the pinch and/or tap. Don't wait to see whether the pup is going to sit or not. The object here is to "super-condition" a response.

We use the command "sit" with a gesture to get pup to stay initially.

46

Same command with variation on gesture.

Do 8 or 10 of the "sits" with pinches and taps. Then give pup his happy dummies and put him up.

LESSON 8

Take pup from kennel and give him his happy dummies. Heel him around a bit and do 10 or 15 "sits" with taps, gradually increasing the intensity from light to moderate taps with the stick. Then give him his happy dummies and put him up.

LESSON 9

Take pup from kennel and give him his happy dummies. Heel him around a bit and give him a few "sits" with light to moderate taps. Then give him a "sit" with a real stinger of a tap. Then 2 or 3 "sits" with light to moderate taps. Then a "sit" with another stinger. In all, you want 10 or 15 "sits" with light to moderate taps intercepted with 2 or 3 stingers.

Next give pup a "sit" with no tap. Move away three steps. If he starts to get up, show him the stick. If he still wants to get up and follow you, then give him a tap with the intensity required to keep him sitting in place as you back off the three steps.

A word of caution. Don't let pup creep. Some pups like to inch toward you as you step away. Let pup know on the front end that this is not allowed. Some pups can turn this creeping into a perverse and plaguing game.

Now that you're 3 steps away from pup, pause for a couple of seconds and then give him the command "here" followed immediately by a light pinch (you had the rope in your hand still, didn't you?). Repeat this 5 or 6 times, then the happy dummies and back in kennel.

We want a vigorous, snappy response to the command "Here."

LESSON 10

First, the happy dummies. Then a bit of heeling drill and some "sits." Now we'll change the schedule on reinforcing "sit." Give pup a pinch or tap not with every "sit" command, but on a intermittent basis. We want the pup to start thinking that he can avoid the pinch or tap if he sits quickly enough.

Next, do 6 or 8 "sit/stays" with the handler moving away from the sitting-in-place pup. Note that I labeled the action "sit/stay" while the only command we use is "sit." This is for two reasons.

First, "sit" is now a somewhat conditioned command and has some meaning to and elicits a response from pup. "Stay" presently means nothing to him.

Second, "stay" is a superfluous command. Pup should sit when so commanded, and remain sitting until released or commanded to do something else.

However, if you wish to use the command "stay," please do so. But wait until pup is staying consistently (lesson 15) before you start using the verbal command "stay."

As you go through the sequence of 6 to 8 "sit/stays," gradually lengthen the distance a step at a time that you move away from pup. Also, gradually increase the duration of pause a second or two each time.

Then the happy dummies and back to the kennel.

LESSON 11

Take pup from kennel and give him his fun dummies. Heel him around a bit and do a few "sits" with intermittent taps. Do 10 or 12 "sit/stay/here" sequences, not forgetting to give the light pinch immediately after the command "here." Keep increasing the distance you move away and the

Happy dummies after each obedience lesson. Don't forget the breaking signal.

48

length of pause. If pup comes before being commanded to do so, then move to meet him with a tap across the chest. Drag him by the pinch collar firmly back to where he should be. Move back to your former position, and again pause. Then give the command "here" followed by a pinch. When he gets to you, command "sit." Then reward him with petting and/or verbal praise depending on his personality.

When you need a longer rope to accommodate your increased distance, put it on pup.

When you've completed your 10 or 12 correct repetitions, give pup his happy dummies and then back to the kennel.

LESSON 12
Repeat lesson 11.

LESSON 13
Repeat lesson 11.

LESSON 14
Repeat lesson 11.

LESSON 15
Repeat lesson 11.

LESSON 16
Repeat lesson 11.

LESSON 17
Repeat lesson 11.

LESSON 18
Repeat lesson 11.

Now we're going to change the fun dummy routine a bit. We'll start adding a little control onto the retrieves. We'll start holding pup a bit before allowing him to retrieve.

Take pup from kennel at heel with your rope attached to his *regular* leather collar. Sit him in the heel position. Do *not* give him the breaking signal, "Hup! Hup! Hup!" Hold the rope tightly in such a manner that pup can feel tension on the collar. Throw the dummy, while simultaneously commanding "sit." When dummy is at the top of its arc, release pup with the command "back." Repeat this once.

Now do several repetitions of your "sit/stay/here" drill with pinch collar. Next we'll add a new twist. Pup should now be sitting in place while you walk off 20 or 30 feet. Sit pup, walk off 20 feet and then command "here." When he's halfway to you, command "sit" while raising the stick in a threatening gesture and stepping toward him. As soon as he sits, give a hand clap, a loud playful "atta boy, what a good dog" to bring him on to you. Then give him some petting and praise.

If he doesn't sit on the command with gesture and step, then continue on to meet him with a crack across the chest with the stick. Repeat as many times as necessary to get him sitting on the gesture.

Do 8 or 10 repetitions of stopping him halfway on the command "sit" with gesture. After the halfway "sit," bring

Happy dummies in the water are great for pup. "HUP, HUP, HUP..." Then move away from the water for the obedience lesson.

him on to you with the praise. This halfway sit, which after lesson 22 we'll cue with a whistle blast instead of the voice command, has two purposes. It's going to increase pup's responsiveness to you, and later on, it will be used in conjuction with training pup on hand signals and blind retrieves.

To end, give him two retrieves in the same manner as we began this lesson. Then back to the kennel.

LESSON 19
Repeat lesson 18. Keep using the gesture to sit him at the halfway point, even if you don't need it. We're going to need it later.

LESSON 20
Repeat lesson 19.

LESSON 21
Repeat lesson 19.

LESSON 22
Repeat lesson 19 with a few variations.

On the retrieves hold pup until the dummy hits the ground. On the halfway "sits," follow the verbal command immediately with a single whistle blast and keep using the threatening gesture. You should also be gradually increasing the distance for the halfway sit.

At this point, you should bring him to you from the halfway sit with the command "here" instead of the hand clap and praise. But change to the command only when he's already coming from the halfway sit with vigor. At this point you should also start increasing the duration of the halfway sit.

crowe '89
Young Black Duck

LESSON 23
Repeat lesson 22.

LESSON 24
Repeat lesson 22.

LESSON 25
Repeat lesson 22.

LESSON 26
Repeat lesson 22 with one variation. Eliminate the verbal command, "sit," for the halfway sit. Give him the single whistle blast in conjunction with the threatening gesture to sit him at the 1/2 way point.

If you wish to condition him to come on a whistle signal, pick one other than the single "sit" blast, such as "tweet-a-tweet" or a trill.

For several lessons, follow up immediately the command "here" with the chosen whistle signal, then use the whistle signals interchangeably with "here." Through association, pup's come response will transfer to the chosen whistle signal.

On the retrieves you should gradually, a couple of seconds at a time, increase the pause before releasing pup with the command "back."

old Canvas
Training Dummy—

Keep holding him with tension on the rope. You don't want to steady him just yet, so don't be in a hurry. It'll be easier later.

LESSON 27

Repeat lesson 26.

LESSON 28

Repeat lesson 26.

LESSON 29

Repeat lesson 26.

LESSON 30

Repeat lesson 26.

LESSON 31

Repeat lesson 26.

LESSON 32

Repeat lesson 26.

Pup should now be fairly obedient and ready for our next phase. Be sure he's still wearing that rope. We don't want to give him the opportunity to learn that when it's off, he's beyond your control. Remember, we're training by habit formation.

Chapter 6
The Conditioned Retrieve

Do you want your pup to be one who always delivers to hand, never drops a bird, never exhibits a hard mouth, never refuses to retrieve, is super persistent in his hunt for that difficult bird, is exceptionally easy to steady, and a model student for blinds and hand signals?

If your answer is yes to all the above, then I have just the program for you. It's called the conditioned retrieve. Just as we conditioned the controlled response of coming, heeling, sitting, and staying, so we also will condition the responses of retrieving. This process will make an average dog good and a good dog, great.

This conditioning of the retrieve response will begin with teaching pup to "turn off" an uncomfortable pinch on his foot by fetching a wooden dowel from your hand. Then, by successive approximation, this response will be extended to the point that pup is fetching 16 feet to right or left on command and a hand signal. He'll also be fetching with direction and purpose 16 feet on a line.

Thus, this conditioned retrieve process in addition to its other benefits will give us the basic elements of blinds and hand signals.

To some it may seem a bit strange to condition the retrieve, something that pup already does, but it's really quite logical. Pup probably already knows how to sit on command before we conditioned the sit response. However, prior to conditioning, he probably only sat on command when he felt like it. After the conditioning, he sits consistenly on command. The conditioning gave the handler vastly greater control of the response.

We want this same control of the retrieve response. Although pup is going to retrieve at any opportunity by instinct, the handler, having more control of the retrieve response, is going to make it much easier to program pup on when not to retrieve. The conditioned retrieve is going to make pup dramatically easier to steady. The relatively mild stimulus we use to condition the retrieve is going to eliminate a whole lot of the force and trauma traditionally associated with steadying pup. The conditioned retrieve process is going to result in a pup who is 70% steady simply by virtue of this process. Additionally, this program is going to give us a pup more amenable to learning to stop on a whistle for hand signals.

If all the above isn't enough, the conditioned retrieve is going to give us much more. It's going to channel pup's excess energy into retrieving by focusing his intensity on getting that bird. He'll spend less time sniffing bushes and more time actively seeking the bird. It will speed up the lazy retriever and temper the wild Indian. It results in a pup who is retrieving for you rather than for himself.

It produces a pup who doesn't drop birds in embarrassing places, such as on the other side of the river. It produces a pup who always delivers tenderly to hand, and one who never develops a hard mouth, because the conditioned retrieve transfers the ownership of the bird from pup to you, the handler. Last but not least, the pup with conditioned retrieve, on exiting the water, will generally not shake until you've taken the bird. Thus, as I'll describe in the water training program, we have a mechanism to promote a relatively "less wet" situation for the best hunt.

In short, I think the conditioned retrieve is the best thing since nickel beer. If there is a magic trick for retriever training, this is it. The conditioned retrieve is magic in the transformation that it induces in pup. It is not magic in terms of time and effort on the part of the trainer. Our basic rules of repetition and consistency still apply.

The conditioned retrieve should not be started until pup is 7 or 8 months old, retrieving confidently, and well conditioned to be obedient. The obedience training is a definite prerequisite for pup, so that he has learned to accept physical restraint and so that he's educated in escape responses.

My preferred method is one I learned from Delmar Smith, the great Oklahoma bird dog trainer. By this method you put pup on a table and do all the training there. The table is used for several reasons. The most important is that it puts pup off balance psychologically and decreases his resistance to training. Additionally, the table allows the trainer to stand comfortably while having complete control of the pup. This goes a long way toward preventing lost tempers accompanied by abuse of pup.

While pup is engaged in the conditioned retrieve program, he should get no other retrieving. There are several reasons for this.

Get pup running vigorously up and down the table accompanied by our breaking signal "HUP. . HUP. . HUP." Don't forget to end every lesson with this.

It gives him no alternative fun behavior with which to contrast the control training. Thus, he'll accept the regimen more readily and it will "take" more completely. You might compare this to a kid who isn't particularly fond of school. If you periodically let him go to the movies instead of school, then it's going to take a lot longer for him to start liking school.

Additionally, field retrieving during the conditioned retrieve program is going to put pup in the position of being able to refuse you while you're trying to train him not to refuse. Whenever he drops or spits out a dummy, he is detraining himself. You could end up going backwards.

Field retrieving during this time can lead to traumatic confrontations in the field that aren't good for pup and are not necessary. Suppose pup spits out a dummy in the field, and you command him to fetch and he doesn't. You'll probably lose your temper and regret it later. The solution is not to give him the opportunity to disobey until he's so well conditioned that he won't disobey.

Thus, while the conditioned retrieve program is in progress, give pup no field training.

To start with, you need a table about waist high, four feet wide, and eight to sixteen feet long. (Preferably sixteen feet long.) Two 4 x 8 sheets of plywood laid end to end on strong supports make an excellent training table. Next, a smooth wire cable should be stretched lengthwise 30″ above the table in such a way that pup can be fastened to it in trolley fashion and be free to run up and down the table.

The next items required are six or seven swivel snaps like those used on the end of a leash. Connected to the cable and then to each other, they will make a chain that hangs down from the cable and attaches to pup's collar. The length of this chain can be adjusted by adding or removing snaps.

LESSON 1

Put pup on the table, fastening the chain from his collar (not a chain choker but a leather or nylon collar) to the cable in a short enough manner that he can not lie down but is free to move up and down the table. Leave him there until he's fairly comfortable and not frightened of being up there. Encourage him to move up and down the table by moving back and forth the length of the table while giving him great encouragement to follow you. Your objective is for him to enjoy running back and forth from each end of the table. This is important because you'll use it to end each session on a happy note.

If you can't get him to do it, encourage him by pulling him from end to end a few times with a lead attached to the swivel to show him that it won't hurt him. Then go back to the encouragement. Again, have him running vigorously and happily from end to end before you continue. This may take three or four sessions but it is well worth the time spent.

Pup is anchored at one end and taught to accept the dowel. If it takes both hands to keep it in his mouth then use both.

56

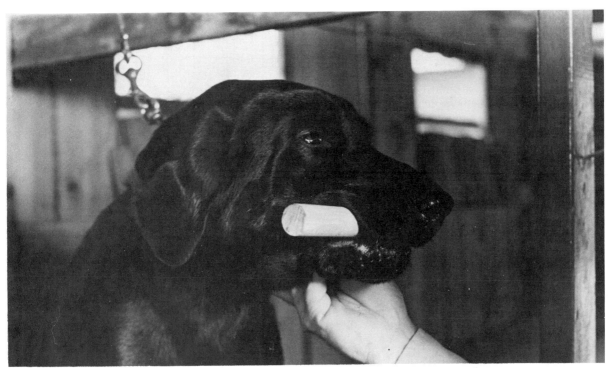

Some don't like it as well as others.

LESSON 2

You'll perform the initial conditioned retrieve with an eight inch long piece of wooden dowel about one inch in diameter. The reason for this is that any bad feeling will be associated with the dowel and not with a training dummy or a bird. We'll bring those in later when pup has begun to accept the training.

Put pup on the table and run him up and down it a bit with an accompanying "HUP — HUP — HUP" to encourage him. Then anchor him at one end of the table, also chaining him short enough so he can't lie down. Hook two fingers of your left hand through his collar. Put the dowel in his mouth with your right hand and hold it there until he quits struggling and trying to spit it out. Pull up the upper lip flap to insure that he's not pinching his lip between teeth and dowel. This lip check should be automatic every time he has the dowel in his mouth; if he's pinching a lip, the discomfort will counteract the behavior we're promoting, that of holding the dowel without opposition.

Pet him soothingly when he's sitting quietly with a dowel in his mouth, with or without you supporting his lower jaw, using the thumb of your left hand to push up under his chin. Repeat this process five or six times and he'll probably be holding the dowel by himself. The reason for the petting and praise when he's sitting quietly is that you want him to feel good when the dowel is in his mouth. This will increase his desire to grab and hold it.

You probably noticed that I didn't use any commands other than "sit" at this point. As with the dummies and birds, we must avoid any bad association with the command "fetch," so we will introduce the "fetch" command after pup is already fetching.

The problems you are most likely to encounter here are: 1) Pup will be jumping around so much you can't hold him. The solution is the command "sit." If this doesn't work then the obedience hasn't been sufficiently instilled. Do more obedience drills on and off the table until you get the proper response to the sit command. 2) Pup develops lock-jaw and you can't get that dowel in his mouth. The solution is to push his gum against a tooth hard enough to open his mouth. Then put the dowel in.

Don't forget to pet soothingly and praise gently when the dowel is in his mouth and he's not fighting it. You want him to feel good while he's holding the dowel. To end the session, run him excitely up and down the table several times with a few "HUP's."

A note of caution: This step of getting pup to sit quietly with the dowel in his mouth, not fighting it and not actively trying to spit it out, is one which is extremely important. As we got the "fight" out of his neck before the obedience training so we must get the "fight" out of his mouth before proceeding with the conditioned retrieve training. As an absolute minimum you must get pup to sit 1½ minutes with dowel in his mouth, not struggling. You may hold him by the collar and prop up his lower jaw with your thumb. That is acceptable, but keep doing it until he'll sit that 1½ minutes, three times in succession without struggling to spit out the dowel.

If you have a difficult pup, I'll give you two further suggestions. Never let him succeed in spitting out the dowel the first time. This will cause him to accept the inevitable more readily. If he's struggling so hard that you have a lot of trouble winning, then use your hand instead of the dowel. Put a leather glove on your right hand and while holding his collar with your left hand, put the right hand in his mouth palm down so that your fingers firmly grasp his lower jaw. He can't spit that hand out. Hold it thus until he quits struggling and swallows, indicating that he's accepted the hand. Then while keeping the hand in his mouth, stroke him soothingly for a minute or so. Repeat two more times and then end the session with an excited run up and down the table. For the next lesson repeat the process with the dowel.

Let me now say a bit about the duration and frequency of sessions. A lot of pups are not going to like this program in the beginning. Therefore, from here on you'll have to exercise some judgement as to how many sessions per day to do and how long to make the sessions. If your pup's reaction is to become a bit sullen, and he's obviously doing it begrudgingly, then one session per day of short duration (5 min.) is plenty; as he gets happier and snappier and begins accepting the program, you can increase frequency and duration of the sessions if you wish. If you don't have the time, then one

"Ruddy"
One of the smartest
of the Diving Ducks

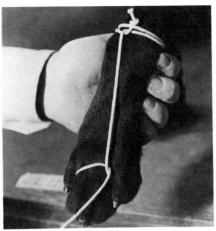

Here's the magic string with a clove hitch above "wrist" joint and half hitch around two middle toes.

session per day is still fine. One further point on the reluctant, sullen pup is to restrict all other activities except the conditioned retrieve training. Keep him in the kennel when he's not on the training table. This will tend to influence him toward earlier acceptance.

LESSON 3

Here you will introduce the negative conditioning stimulus. Put pup on the table and run him up and down a few times. Then anchor him at one end, tied short enough that he can't lie down. Take a piece of twine about 1/8th inch diameter and tie a clove hitch around pup's foreleg above the "wrist." Run the string on down to his toes where you place a half hitch around his middle two toes. You should have about 2½ feet of string hanging from the half hitch at his toes. This is what you pull to pinch his foot.

Now comes the *critical* part. You're going to give him that first pinch while holding the dowel two inches from his mouth. You must quickly establish that the pinch is relieved by getting the dowel in his mouth. On the first pinch you'll get one of several reactions:

1) He'll open his mouth to protest in which case you stick the dowel in and release the pinch simultaneously. Then quickly slip two fingers through his collar under the neck and prop up his chin with the thumb of the same hand to keep him from spitting it out. Pet him soothingly and praise gently as he holds the dowel. Then take it from him with a command of "leave it" or "drop." You'll notice that you don't use the command "fetch" here, and won't until he's already fetching with vigor. We don't want the command "fetch," associated with fear or confusion.

2) He'll get lockjaw, in which case you pinch a little harder. If this doesn't get his mouth open then you will have to. With one hand push his gum against a tooth to open his mouth while pushing the dowel in. This requires a little manual dexterity but you can do it. When it's in his mouth, release the pinch. Pet and praise while he's holding it. Take the dowel out of his mouth with the command "leave it" or "drop." Six or eight repetitions should get the idea across.

3) He'll try to bite the string where it is pinching his foot in which case you let him bite the dowel and finish as described above.

4) He'll dance around so much you can't get the dowel even close to his mouth. The solution here is again the command "sit." If it doesn't work, then he's not obedient enough. Go back to the obedience drills on and off the table.

After several repetitions of having the dowel in his mouth turn off the pinch, pup will begin to get the idea. Then he'll start reaching for the dowel when he feels the pinch. When he has done this eight or ten times you can end the session. Again do this by running him up and down the table with vigor and enthusiasm so he is happy when he is put back in his kennel.

A word here about the technique of the pinch. Keep it relatively light here on the front end. Pup is in a strange

Learning that fetching the dowel turns off the pinch.

situation and probably feeling uneasy. You want to induce discomfort with the pinch, but you don't want to panic him. You want to establish the proper escape response, fetching the dowel, with the stimulus at a low level. Don't be in a hurry. Your manner should be calm and deliberate. You may have to physically pry his mouth open and put in the dowel several times with the accompanying "turn off" of the pinch. Then you may have to apply the light pinch for a duration of two or three minutes to get the first voluntary fetch. Take all the time you need. The critical fact is to establish the escape response without scaring pup. After the escape response is established, we'll address shaping and making it snappy.

LESSON 4

Here you will introduce the command "fetch" and gradually increase the distance pup is reaching for the dowel.

Put pup on the table and run him up and down a few times. Anchor him at one end, tied short enough that he cannot lie down. Do about five fetches with pinches, the pinch only hard enough to elicit a rapid response. If he's still trying to spit out the dowel, then keep reaching up with your left hand to slip two fingers under his collar and prop up the lower jaw with your thumb. This spitting out behavior will damp out after a few lessons.

Now add on the command "fetch." Your sequence will be "fetch," pinch, response. Repeat this 10 times. Then end the session with the table running.

LESSON 5

Repeat Lesson 4 but add a snap or two to the cable and hold the dowel closer to table top so that pup will be reaching further to grab the dowel. Do 10 or 15 repetitions with the verbal command "fetch" which we'll keep using now. Don't forget to begin and end the sessions with vigorous running up and down the table.

If pup wants to lie down when you lengthen his chain, then he probably didn't get enough familiarization time on the table prior to Lesson 2. Start over again from the beginning and use more petting. If you try this and don't eliminate the lying down then stay on Lesson 4 until pup does stop the lying down.

LESSON 6

Repeat Lesson 4 adding snaps and extending the reaching distance for pup to the point that you're holding the dowel just off the table. After your 10 to 15 repetitions of the fetch sequence add a new twist. Now hold the dowel a foot or two off to the side opposite the half-hitched toes. If the string is on his left leg then hold the dowel to his right side. Give him the command "fetch" and a pinch toward the dowel. We want him to take a couple of steps to get to the dowel.

I might mention here that you should try to watch yourself on shoving the dowel toward his mouth. The desired response is pup chasing the dowel and not the reverse. Do about 5 repetitions of this and then end the session in the prescribed manner.

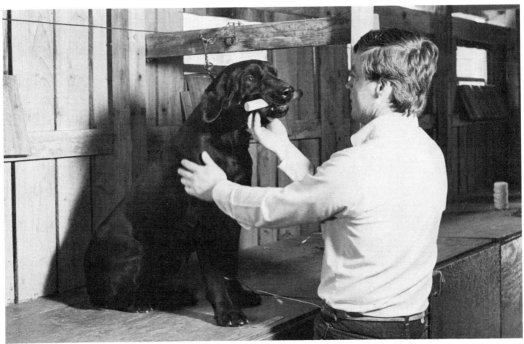

After the pinch it's sit quietly and hold it while trainer praises and pets soothingly.

61

Reaching a little further to get that dowel.

LESSON 7

Repeat Lesson 6 but reverse directions. If you were having pup fetch to the left, this time go right. When you reverse direction, change the string over to the opposite foot so that you are pinching the pup's right foot for pup to go to his left. This is for two reasons. First, pup needs to have both

We're nearly to the table top now.

sides trained in order for the job to be complete, and second, pup won't get a foot tangled by having to step across the string. End in the prescribed manner.

A reminder: You should still be petting pup soothingly at the end of each fetch sequence when he's sitting quietly, holding the dowel.

Just about now you may be one of a chosen few who is recognizing that he's got a hardcase to deal with. Your particular pup is still trying to spit that */*?#'! dowel out instead of sitting quietly and holding it like our angelic textbook model. By now he should realize what's desired; after all you've demonstrated by holding the dowel in his mouth about 80 times in the past 6 lessons. If he's not cooperating by now it's probably not from lack of knowledge. It's what I call avoidance behavior or refusal to accept the training. It's time for a little remedial drill for these few recalcitrants.

Anchor pup at one end of the table, tied up short enough that he can't lie down. Command "fetch," give a pinch and offer him the dowel, but don't let go of it. Now every time he takes his mouth off of the dowel you're holding, give him a good pinch, accompanied by silence. When the pinch gets his mouth back around the dowel immediately release the pinch. After the initial command "fetch" you should say nothing and do no petting. We're teaching this rebellious pup that it is his responsibility to hold that dowel after the initial fetch. A few 10 minute sessions of this procedure of pain when the dowel is out of his mouth

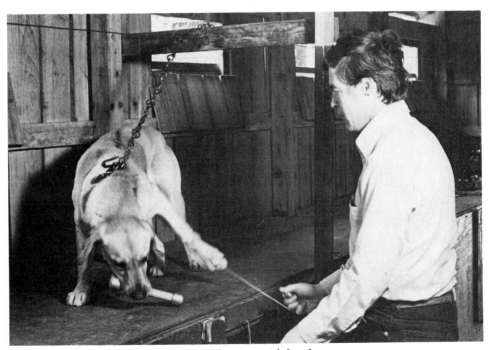

Here's the first fetch of a dowel not held in someone's hand.

contrasted with the absence of pain when the dowel is in his mouth will generally straighten out the delinquent.

One further refinement that some few masters of avoidance behavior will pull is a game of chicken. During the fetching, this pup will try to grab that dowel as close as possible to the hand that's holding it. Their object seeming to be to bluff you into holding it gingerly with your fingertips and then not at all. The solution here is to call his bluff. Wrap your whole hand around one end of the dowel and present a large target. Present the dowel thus held with a "fetch" and a firm pinch. Invariably this will solve the problem. I've done this with literally hundreds of dogs and have not had one grab the hand yet. However, I would not recommend this procedure for a 2 or 3 year old Chesapeake.

LESSON 8

For these subsequent lessons, we'll go to a dowel that is wrapped with tape at both ends so that its shape resembles that of a dumbell with the middle portion resting about ½ inch above the tabletop. Put pup on the table. Run him up and down a couple of times. Anchor him at one end with enough slack that he can reach a dowel on the table top. Do 4 or 5 fetch sequences with the dowel resting on the tabletop but with your hand touching the end of it as if holding it. This seems to be a tough transition for pup to go through; from taking the dowel from your hand as opposed to fetching it off the tabletop when no hand is attached.

Next put the dowel on the table and withdraw the hand. Then do your fetch sequence. You may have to hold the pinch a bit longer or pinch a bit harder than usual to get

Now we're going half the table length with speed, vigor, and purpose. Note hand signal from trainer.

Then back to starting point to sit and hold before delivering.

through this transition, but do so if needed. Let pup learn that the only escape route lies in fetching the dowel. After a few repetitions, pup will give in and you can then lighten up. Do 8 or 10 repetitions and then finish with the table run.

LESSON 9

Put pup on the table and run him up and down a few times. Do 8 or 10 repetitions of your fetch sequence at one end of the table, with pup fetching from the tabletop. Then put pup at the other end of the table, change the cord to the other foot, and do 8 or 10 more repetitions. Finish with the table running.

LESSON 10

Put pup on the table and run him up and down a few times. Do 5 repetitions of the fetch sequence as in Lesson 9. For the 6th "fetch," put the dowel on the table about 2 feet down the table from where pup is sitting. As you give the command "fetch" with a light pinch, give a hand signal and take a step or two in that direction. Your pinch should still be coupled with the command "fetch," but should have tapered off by now to being fairly light while still eliciting a rapid positive response. Also, pup should be sitting quietly until you command "fetch" and follow with the pinch. Don't let him anticipate your command as he will probably be prone to do. After he's fetched the dowel, he should return to the starting point, sit and hold the dowel until you take it. If he isn't returning smartly to the starting point, give a pull on that string tied to his foot and the command "here." However, if you've been doing the table running exercise consistently he should be well cued to moving with you. Thus as you give a "fetch" command for down the table you should move snappily also, staying ahead of pup. In the same manner you should return to the starting point. You should continue this moving with pup, staying a bit in front of him, for several lessons. Do 5 fetches in this manner and finish with the table running.

Chesapeake Bay Retriever—"Gal" 1983

LESSON 11

Put pup on table and repeat Lesson 10. The direction that pup is moving for his fetch should be the same. Don't forget to move with him as explained in Lesson 10. Also don't let him anticipate the command "fetch." He should sit until commanded to fetch. This bit of behavior will be used later in steadying. If he is anticipating your command simply hold on to the string and let him hit the end of it. Then bring him back to his former position and let him sit a few seconds before commanding "fetch" (accompanied by hand signal and step in the appropriate direction).

Increase the distance that pup is traversing to 4 feet and then to 6 feet doing 5 to 6 repetitions for each distance. Then finish with the table running.

LESSON 12

Put pup on table and do 4 "fetches" traversing 6 feet of table, then 4 at 8 feet, then 4 at 10 feet, then 4 at 12 feet. Keep the direction the same. Finish as before.

LESSON 13

Continue as in Lesson 12, increasing the distance in 2 foot increments to 16 feet which should be the length of the table. Do 4 or 5 fetches the full length of the table. Finish as before.

LESSON 14

Do 6 "fetches" the length of the table, in the same direction as before. Then put your string on pup's other foot and starting from the opposite end of the table, change directions. Give him 3 "fetches" to the midway point and then 4 or 5 traversing the full length. Then finish with the table running.

LESSON 15

Do 6 "fetches" in each direction. Keep moving with pup on the "fetches," not letting him anticipate. Also maintain the requirement to return to his starting point, sit, and deliver to hand. Finish with the table running.

LESSON 16

Repeat Lesson 15. To save yourself some walking, you can place up to 6 dowels at the end of the table spaced far enough apart that pup can't easily pick up 2 at once and have him fetch them successively. If he does try to pick up 2 at once, as he's reaching for the second one, you should pull his string and command "here." Let him know that he's only to pick one at a time.

LESSON 17

Repeat Lesson 15.

LESSON 18

Repeat Lesson 15. You should now be able to stop moving up and down the table with pup on his fetches and he should be going without the pinch. You should be able to stand at one end of the table, in front of pup, give him the command fetch with a hand signal and step in the appropriate direction. He, in response, should snappily and willingly run to the other end, fetch the dowel, return to you, sit and deliver to hand.

If he does this, proceed. If not, then keep repeating Lesson 15 until he does, and then proceed.

LESSON 19

Now we're going to introduce the training dummy. Put pup on the table and tie him up short. Hold the training dummy near pup's mouth and command "fetch" followed with a pinch. Pet him while he's holding it and then take it.

Repeat five times. then give him enough slack to fetch it off the table top and do 5 repetitions of same. Then do 6 "fetches" the length of the table in each direction. Move with pup on these so you'll be in place to prevent a refusal should one seem imminent. Then finish with table running.

LESSON 20

Do 6 fetches of each direction, the full length of the table, using dummies. Finish with table running.

LESSON 21

Repeat Lesson 20.

LESSON 22

Repeat Lesson 20.

LESSON 23

Repeat Lesson 20. Also we'll start conditioning pup's ear here. After you've done your 6 fetches in each direction then tie pup up short. Put 4 fingers of the left hand under pup's collar. Lay his ear over the collar. With your thumbnail press the ear against the collar. This will be the ear pinch.

This ear pinch should only be given when you have a hold on the collar. Then you can be assured that the desired response, fetching, is going to turn off the pinch. If you don't have the collar then the undesirable response of jumping away and pulling the ear out of grasp is the one that will be rewarded by the cessation of the pinch. This jumping away response, incidentally, is also an excellent building block for teaching pup to run away from you.

Hold the dummy within pup's reach, command "fetch," and give the ear pinch. The magnitude of pinch will vary. Use whatever it takes to get a speedy response. Repeat 6 times. Then lengthen pup's chain and give him 6 fetches with ear pinches to fetch the dummy off the table top. Finish with table running.

Black Duck Decoy—
Solid Cork—(Over Sized)
Typical Eastern Shore—

LESSON 24

Repeat Lesson 23 but make all the ear pinch fetches on dummies lying on the table top. Thus pup will do six fetches in each direction, the length of the table, followed by 6 fetches with the ear pinch. Then finish with the table run.

This is the ear pinch used for the transition from the table to the ground. Note: hold the dummy off the ground first. Note also that hand on pup's collar. We want escape from the pinch to be in fetching the dummy, not in shying away from trainer.

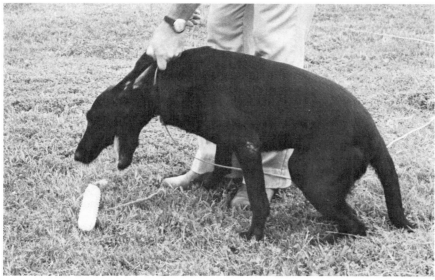

Then from the ground. Note the trainer always has pup by the collar when pinch occurs.

The pinch is immediately released upon pup's fetching the dummy.

LESSON 25
Repeat Lesson 24.

LESSON 26
Repeat Lesson 24

LESSON 27
Repeat Lesson 19 but use frozen pigeons instead of dummies.

LESSON 28
Repeat Lesson 23 using frozen pigeons instead of dummies.

LESSON 29
Repeat Lesson 24 using frozen pigeons.

LESSON 30
Repeat Lesson 24 using frozen pigeons.

LESSON 31
Repeat Lesson 19 using freshly killed pigeons.

LESSON 32
Repeat Lesson 23 using freshly killed pigeons.

LESSON 33
Repeat Lesson 24 using freshly killed pigeons.

LESSON 34
Repeat Lesson 19 using frozen ducks.

LESSON 35
Repeat Lesson 23 using frozen ducks.

LESSON 36
Repeat Lesson 24 using frozen ducks.

LESSON 37
Repeat Lesson 24 using frozen ducks.

LESSON 38
Repeat Lesson 19 using dead unfrozen ducks.

LESSON 39
Repeat Lesson 23 using dead unfrozen ducks. Repeat Lesson 24 using dead unfrozen ducks.

LESSON 40
Repeat Lesson 24 using training dummies.

LESSON 41
Repeat Lesson 24 using training dummies.

LESSON 42
Repeat Lesson 24 using dummies. Then we'll try pup on the ground. Take him off the table, attach leash, sit him and do two or three fetches with ear pinch of a dummy held in front of him. Then have him fetch it, with command and pinch, off the ground 5 or 6 times. Then put him in the kennel.

LESSON 43
Take pup from kennel, attach leash so you'll be assured of retaining control. Give pup 8 or 10 fetches of dummies on the ground. Continue to give a pinch with each fetch.

LESSON 44
Repeat Lesson 43. Then try a "fetch" without the pinch. You should get the proper response. If you don't, continue repeating Lesson 43 until you do.

If after 5 or 6 more repetitions of Lesson 43 you are still not getting the proper response with the verbal command alone, then you've got a hardhead. We'll change the technique a bit for him. Grasp collar and command "fetch." Pinch ear firmly, but don't let pup get the dummy. Hold him off by the collar for 10 to 15 seconds while continuing the firm pinch and repeating the command fetch. Then let him grab it. A few lessons using this technique will generally increase the incentive of the hardhead.

LESSON 45
If you've now got pup fetching off the ground consistently on just the verbal command then you're nearly through. The finishing touch is to force pup to go a bit. To do this put 6 or 8 dummies scattered closely together on the ground. Back away with pup to a distance of 3 or 4 feet and with the command "fetch" and a pinch, send pup for them in succession.

LESSON 46
Repeat Lesson 45 but back up 6 to 8 feet from the dummies.

LESSON 47
Repeat Lesson 46 backing up a few more feet but using the command "back" instead of "fetch."

LESSON 48
Repeat Lesson 47.

Sailing Greenhead looking for Company—

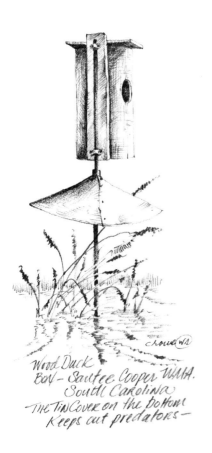

Wood Duck
Box – Santee Cooper WMA.
South Carolina
The Tin Cover on the Bottom
Keeps out predators –

Congratulations, pup should now be thoroughly conditioned on the retrieve. If you've done the obedience and conditioned retrieve training properly then pup is now 80% trained. Not only is he obedient and conditioned on the retrieve, but he's also got the behavior patterns well started for steadiness, lining, and hand signals. The hard part is behind you and pup.

Chapter 7
Steadying

Nothing is more pleasant than a properly trained retriever that sits quietly at heel while you are shooting ducks, and then upon command charges out to make the required retrieves. This property of sitting quietly until commanded to retrieve is termed "steadiness." The lack of it is one of the most commonly observed faults in retrievers.

In addition to making your hunt more enjoyable, the steady dog runs less risk of being deafened or shot by one of your hunting companions shooting cripples.

The proper time to begin steadying your pup is after he is obedience trained and conditioned on the retrieve. These two phases of the training process establish the basic behavior patterns for steadiness. The obedience training instills in pup the habit of obeying the commands, "heel," "sit," and "stay" in the face of ordinary distractions and the general excitement which accompanies shooting ducks from a blind or boat. The conditioned retrieve process conditions pup in the behavior pattern of sit, and then, fetch on command, which is the basic behavior pattern of steadiness.

What we must do now is take this behavior and mold it in such a way that pup is reliable even in the most tempting of circumstances. The magic trick to steadying your dog is to never let pup succeed with his retrieve when he breaks, i.e. retrieves *without a command* from you.

Never let him be rewarded with the bird or dummy when he breaks. To avoid this, always run him with his check cord on and held in your hand. We want to be sure that he understands what you want, and we don't want to dampen his enthusiasm, so the steadying must be done gradually. You don't want to immediately go out and throw a dummy or bird for your young pup and have him flip end over end while you're holding on to a 15 foot cord. Your pup will think you are punishing him for retrieving and he may decide that it is not worth running to that bird just to have you jerk his neck off. Pup must have prior conditioning so he can make the distinction between being corrected for retrieving as opposed to being corrected for retrieving *with out the command.*

After completing the conditioned retrieve program, you should give pup a week or two of retrieving to loosen him up. Do this with pup trailing a check cord by which you can hold him for a few seconds before releasing him with the command "back." Also upon his return, require him to heel, sit, and deliver to hand. It is also a good idea to throw in a few obedience drills during this time. Give him plenty of retrieves on land and water and then we're ready to start the steadying process.

It is very hard to lay out a precise lesson plan for this phase. Some dogs will come out of the conditioned retrieve training 90% steady and some 20%, with variations in between, so I'll give you a lesson plan for the 50-50 dog. Then you will have to either extend or shorten the lesson plan, depending on the results you're getting from your dog.

Another judgement you will have to make according to the nature of your dog is whether to require pup to wear the pinch collar during the following steadying sessions. If he's a tough hard-going individual then you probably will. If your pup is softer and less aggressive, then attach the check cord to his *regular* leather collar.

Flaring Greenhead
Mallard — 1982

Lesson 1 — We'll start pup on the steadying with a drill I call sight blinds. Essentially, this is an extension of the conditioned retrieve process. First, we'll go to a field or yard with short grass where pup can see white dummies lying on the ground from a distance. Then with pup on a check cord and sitting at heel, toss 3 or 4 white training dummies about 30 or 40 feet in front of you in a closely spaced group. Do not release pup to retrieve. Turn and heel him in the opposite direction 10 feet. Then turn back to face the dummies and sit pup at heel. Extend your left hand out over his head to give him a line to the dummies. Pause (make sure your hand is not interfering with his vision) and then send him with the command "back." There is no need to shout here either. He's sitting next to you and can hear quite well. When he returns, have him heel, sit, and deliver to hand. Back up

If pup's not steady and gets out in front of the gun he may be permanently deafened by muzzle blast.

another 10 feet and send him again as before. Back up another 10 feet for each dummy.

You notice that we repeat this sequence only 3 or 4 times. This is because, as in other training drills, we're not only teaching pup to perform the desired behavior sequence, we're also teaching him to like it. Therefore, less is better. We don't want to turn it into a grind.

This exercise has a variety of benefits. As it relates to steadiness, it conditions pup to quite a long pause between seeing the dummies thrown and being commanded to retrieve. That 10 foot walk away after the dummies are down also starts a mental pattern for *remembering* (which will help when you start double and triple retrieves). It also is the basic drill for teaching and conditioning pup to perform blind retrieves.

After pup has picked up the three or four sight blinds, then put him up for the day.

Lesson 2 — Take pup back to the same field and do a few obedience drills. (Here, sit, sit halfway to you on whistle, etc.) Then sit pup at heel in the same place as you did yesterday and toss 3 or 4 white training dummies to the same place as before. This time back up 20 feet before sending him for his first dummy, 10 feet back for the second, and an additional 10 feet for each dummy thereafter. If you're getting any balking, then an ear pinch or two should straighten things out.

Lesson 3 — Repeat Lesson 2, but back up 30 feet for the first retrieve, 40 feet for the second, etc.

Lesson 4 — Repeat Lesson 2, but back up 50 feet for the first retrieve and an additional 10 feet for each subsequent retrieve.

Lesson 5 — Repeat Lesson 2 but back up 60 feet for the first retrieve and then back up in 20 foot increments for each subsequent retrieve.

Lesson 6 — Repeat Lesson 2 but back up 80 feet for the first retrieve and then back up in 20 foot increments for each subsequent retrieve.

Now we've got pup well established on simple sight blinds and lines. This is enough right now for our purpose of making it easier to steady pup. We'll come back to this drill later in teaching pup blind retrieves. However, if you prefer to continue this drill as an adjunct to the lesson plan it will be quite beneficial. I would however recommend it only for those pups that are retrieving quite eagerly. For those that may be lacking a bit in enthusiasm I'd recommend sticking with the lesson plan and keeping the work load light.

Lesson 7 — Take pup out with his check cord on. Do a couple of obedience drills, then sit pup and holding the check cord, step 3 paces in front of pup. Command pup to sit (even though he is already sitting) and toss a dummy 10 ft. in front of you while keeping your eyes on him ready to give the command "Sit" if necessary to keep him there until commanded to retrieve. The reason for standing 3 paces in front of him is to inhibit pup. He'll be less likely to break with you standing between him and the dummy. Similarly the short 10 ft. toss is less enticing to pup than a thirty yard throw. We're trying to stay well below the threshold of excitement that will cause pup to break. That way we can teach him the correct behavior sequence and reward him for it. We want to get across to pup that he's to sit while the dummy is thrown and await your command to retrieve. You want him to learn that when he does this he's rewarded by being allowed to retrieve. This will establish a positive behavior pattern from which we'll later correct deviations with the best chance of pup understanding precisely what is required of him.

Do eight repetitions of this short toss retrieve. If the three paces in front, short toss, and verbal "sit" are not enough to keep pup sitting there, then get out the stick from the obedience drills. As you toss the dummy and command "sit," simultaneously hold up the stick in a threatening gesture. If this doesn't keep him sitting, then you didn't do the obedience training well enough and should go back to obedience drills for a week or so.

When and if pup breaks, you are of course holding the check cord and that'll stop him. At this point sit him back where he started from and *you* walk out and get the dummy. Seeing you do this hurts much more than a physical punishment and has a more lasting effect. Ideally we'd like to have in this lesson, six successful sequences wherein pup's threshold isn't exceeded and he doesn't break. We'd like also one or 2 unsuccessful sequences where pup breaks, is stopped, and watches you pick up the dummy. We'd like to end the lesson with a successful sequence, however.

Early steadying. Stand a couple of steps in front of pup while showing him the stick and commanding "sit" while you toss out a short dummy.

Walking out to start sight blinds. If pup isn't steady he should be wearing collar and check cord.

Sit pup and toss out some dummies in a close group.

Walk back a few yards.

Lesson 8 — Do a few obedience drills. Then do eight or ten more short toss retrieves with you standing in front of pup. Again try to engineer it so that he breaks once or twice and can be stopped and corrected by seeing you pick it up. The breaks may be engineered by pausing longer, not giving a threatening gesture, not standing quite so far in front, or a longer throw. Remember however to end as always with a successful sequence.

Lesson 9 — Repeat Lesson 8.

Lesson 10 — Repeat Lesson 8 but lengthen the throws.

Lesson 11 — Repeat Lesson 8 but lengthen the throws a bit more.

Lesson 12 — Here we'll slightly increase the temptation for pup by introducing him to double retrieves, i.e. have your pup sitting while you throw one dummy in one direction and another dummy about 90 degrees in the other direction and then send the pup on the last dummy down. Hand on check cord and standing in front of pup, throw him a long dummy such that it lands where he can see it. Pause a few seconds and send pup on the retrieve. When he returns take the dummy and as formerly, throw it back to the same spot. Then toss one off to the side (at least 90 degrees), pause and send pup for this short one. After he delivers this to hand and is lined up for the memory retrieve, pause a few seconds for him to orient himself and remember that other dummy. Then send him for it with the command "BACK."

If pup is successful on this first double, repeat it 3 or 4 times and quit. If he's unsuccessful because of breaking then the temptation is too great for him and you need to go back to single throws for a while until he's more steady. If he's unsuccessful because he can't seem to remember that other dummy out there then do the memory retrieve several times as a sight blind and then try the double again.

There are a couple of things that were done on this first double that merit attention. First, the training took place on short grass with white dummies, such that pup could see them lying on the ground thirty or forty yards away. This insures that pup is going to find them quickly. Next you used the "memory bird" as a single retrieve before you used it as a double. This capitalizes on pup's tendency to go back to the same place he's been before. We started building this behavior with the conditioned retrieve training and sight blind exercises. Thirdly, when you used the double, you tossed the second bird out at an angle of at least 90 degrees. This made it easier for pup to differentiate as to which dummy he'd already picked up when you were ready to send him for the "memory bird." In short we engineered the exercise in such a manner that pup would be successful. We now want to develop this behavior into a habit by repetition. What we're developing here with the doubles is both steadiness and a pup that, upon bringing back one bird, is expectant of and anticipating another bird out there.

Give pup a line and send him with the command "back" to retrieve
a dummy.

When he gets back make him sit and deliver to hand.

Then move further away for the next sight blind.

A word of caution on the doubles. Don't fall into the ego trap of wanting to direct pup to the bird (dummy) of your choice. Let him pick which one he wants to retrieve first. Most pups will want the most recently thrown dummy first because that's where their attention is focused. A few will do it in reverse. Either way, let pup pick it. If you feel compelled to select for pup, wait until later when he's well educated on doubles and triples and proficient at lining and handling.

Relating this to hunting, some people feel that pup needs to be taught selection so that you can direct pup to pick up cripples first, but I disagree. Pup will automatically pick up the cripples first because a live moving duck is more exciting and desirable to him than a no-movement dead duck. As he gains hunting experience pup will learn to spot a cripple before it hits the water, and he'll retrieve it first.

Lesson 13: Do an obedience drill. Then do 4 doubles in the same manner and place as lesson 12.

Lesson 14: Repeat lesson 13.

Lesson 15: Repeat lesson 13.

Lesson 16: Repeat lesson 13 with a slight variation. Before you send pup on the retrieve, count to three out loud. We want to teach pup to ignore the sound of your voice and respond only on the command "BACK."

Lesson 17: Repeat lesson 16.

Lesson 18: Repeat lesson 16 but instead of counting out loud, blow a duck call a bit before sending pup to retrieve.

Lesson 19: Repeat lesson 18.

Lesson 20: Do about 5 single retrieves while still standing 2 or 3 steps in front of pup, but still with a hand or foot on the check cord so that you can stop him if necessary. This time we'll use clipwing pigeons for pup to retrieve.

Lesson 21: Repeat lesson 20 using clipwing pigeons and firing a shotgun. Only fire the shotgun this close to pup if he's already been introduced to it. If he hasn't then refer back to Chapter 3, "Raising a Puppy" and properly introduce pup to the shotgun before firing this close to pup.

Lesson 22: Repeat lesson 21.

Lesson 23: Repeat lesson 21.

Lesson 24: Repeat lesson 21.

Pup should now be relatively steady, but keep that check cord on him another month just to make sure. The secret of success in steadying is never let him succeed, i.e. get the bird, when he breaks.

Even after pup is relatively steady you need to stay ahead of him a bit, and anticipate potential misdemeanors. When he's been sitting up for a week or two with no retrieving then he'll probably be somewhat prone to break, so anticipate it and hang that check cord on him. The same applies for the first hunt or two of the season.

Helping pup to stay steady on a longer throw. Watch pup, not the dummy.

Another pitfall to avoid is sending pup too fast. If you start sending him just as the bird hits the water or while it's still falling, then pup will start expecting to be sent fast and then he'll start breaking. So always pause for a bit after the birds are down before sending pup to retrieve them.

Now that pup is steady, fairly civilized, and has some small degree of proficiency on easy doubles, you can start throwing him more marks. Start putting some distance on his retrieves. If you can recruit a helper to put out in the field as your thrower, it would be quite helpful. If not, then a long sight blind will do quite adequately.

Another solution for increased distance is the Retriev-R-Trainer™. This is a hand held apparatus which shoots a training dummy by means of a .22 caliber blank cartridge.

Two cautions are in order using this device. First it's quite hard on your hand when you hold it to shoot. An excellent solution is to buy the shoulder stock offered as an accessory or to make one from a couple of 2 x 2's, clamping the retriever trainer to the homemade stock with a couple of radiator hose clamps.

Another advantage of using the retriever trainer with stock attached is that it is excellent at training pup to look

As pup gets steady, progress to shotguns and birds. Until he's trustworthy, keep him a few feet behind you and keep a foot on that checkcord.

The Retriev-R-Trainer™ mounted on a shoulder stock is an excellent trainer aid.

out in the direction the gun is pointing. This conditioning is quite valuable in speeding up the process of pup learning to see the ducks fall during his first hunts.

Secondly, you need to be careful of extended use of the Retrieve-R-Trainer. Just as too many hand thrown retrieves will get pup hunting at the distance you can throw, so will this device get pup hunting at its own distance of throw where pup's learning by repetition can be detrimental.

Generally, on pup's marking program you must train him to use his eyes by developing his confidence that the bird is where his eyes saw it fall. He's born with a propensity to use his nose but needs some conditioning on the eye use.

The way to achieve this is to make his marks progressively harder such that he usually finds the bird or dummy after only a short hunt. Also, on doubles and later on triples, usually throw the memory bird as a single retrieve and then repeat it with the second and/or third bird added on.

At this stage of training, there are a couple of trainer tendencies which tend to detract from maximum development of pup's potential. One is testing.

Pup is doing well on simple marks, is steady and obedient, and you're very proud of him. Your tendency is to go out and try to prove how great he is by seeing how tough a retrieve he can perform in terms of cover, distance, etc. This *does not* contribute to maximum confidence. You want to train pup to succeed, *not train him to fail.*

Another trainer pitfall which can occur at about this point is a tendency to assume that since he's obedient and steady now, he'll stay that way. So the trainer lets up on the control about now.

That's not the way it works. Pup has learned what to do and is well schooled in it, but he also has a funny little quirk in his nature. Most pups are going to periodically test your control limits. That's the way of pups — and most dogs.

You as the trainer need merely remain consistent in your demands. This lets pup know that the limits are still where they were.

What you don't want to do is let pup start slipping until he exceeds your threshold of tolerance and then punish him for it. It's not his fault. It's yours. You communicated to pup by your laxity that the limits were loosening, therefore he loosened. You can't verbally tell pup what the limits are, so you must demonstrate it by being consistent.

The shoulder stock will help a lot in teaching pup to look where the shotgun is pointing.

Chapter 8
Duck Blinds and Hand Signals

Now that pup is steady, it's time to venture into his advanced work which will include blinds and hand signals. This will consist of teaching pup to go out on a line when he has seen nothing fall, stop on command, cast right or left, or back on command. This will allow us to retrieve those fallen ducks that pup didn't see.

This sounds complicated but it's not. We have already established the basic behavior patterns for this exercise in the obedience and conditioned retrieve training chapter. Now is the time to reinforce and strengthen these patterns and integrate them into the total sequence.

First, let's talk about whether or not pup is ready for his advanced training. If pup has been handled properly through the obedience, conditioned retrieve training, and steadying, he ought to be ready.

In this regard, you might hear a few folks say that pup needs a season of hunting before you start the blinds and hand signals. This is not logical. Bear in mind that at this point pup is pliable, malleable, well conditioned to respond, and paying attention to you and your commands. For many of you this is the time that pup will be more responsive to you than any other stage in his lifetime because, for most owners, the tendency is to back off and get sloppy. So the time to teach hand signals is *now*. To wait until he's had a season of hunting will just make the job harder. Picking up 80 or 100 ducks with no help from you hardly makes him more responsive in learning to accept help from you. That season of hunting might just make the job harder by making pup more independent.

There will be, however, a few exceptions to the norm. These will usually be the pups that are a bit low on retrieving desire, especially in the water. The extra degree of control required for hand signals may further inhibit their retrieving desire. These pups *do need a season of hunting before starting the hand signals.*

What it comes down to is that you the trainer *need* to observe the dog while beginning this phase of training. If he's performing with a fair degree of compliance, then proceed. If he's resisting you every day and you find yourself constantly nagging then you may need to scrap the hand signals until a later date.

Our objective is a pup who will like these hand signals, so we'll engineer the training with that in mind. The training will essentially consist of the continuation of three drills in which pup should be proficient. These are the obedience drill, the conditioned retrieve training drill, and the sight blind drill. We'll keep the distances short, the sessions short and the pace snappy. You'd like to inject as much of an attitude of play as possible, without sacrificing your consistent control. To these ends we'll make the sessions short and for the first several lessons, of no more frequency than once per day.

Initially you'll do only the casting drill which is a continuation of conditioned retrieve training, and do it only once per day until pup is proficient, and enjoying it. Then you can increase the frequency if you wish. Also at this point you'll add on the obedience and sight blind drills and carry them forward concurrently with the casting drill. These three drills are the building blocks from which we'll develop the more complex behavior of blind retrieves.

Let's proceed with pup trailing a check cord for every lesson. You'll need a maximum degree of control from here on, because you *must*, down the line, get pup to *stop* and *sit* when he's thirty yards away and running full bore on a retrieve. Therefore start with and continue with pup trailing the check cord. If yours is a particularly tough customer proceed with pup wearing the pinch collar and check cord.

Lesson 1: First, pup must be fairly automatic on obedience: heeling, sitting, staying. If he's gotten sloppy, then review these lessons a bit before starting the casting drill. Do not allow the casting lesson to deteriorate into an obedience lesson. The casting drill should be started on ground with little or no cover such that the white training dummies will be quite visible to pup.

Banded
Hen Mallard
Ducks Unlimited

Sit pup down and step several paces away from him. Toss two dummies such that they land six or eight feet to the right of pup. Then give him a light single whistle blast to attract his glance. Give him a hand signal toward the dummies with the command "FETCH." When he delivers the dummy give him lots of praise and a pat or two. Then sit him back where he initially was and cast him, again *preceding* the command "FETCH" with a light single whistle blast.

Next repeat this same sequence on two dummies to the left and then dummies straight back away from you, the handler. On the back casts use the command "BACK."

Here are the reasons we're doing it this way: First, we're using short distances (6 to 8 foot casts) because we want pup to do it right and we want him to like it. Then, we'll gradually increase the distances as he increases his proficiency.

We're *preceding* the cast with a single whistle blast in order to condition an association of anxious expectation in pup. We've already trained him to sit on the whistle with the obedience drill. Now we're trying to influence him to like it. This is simply conditioning: Whistle followed by *cast,* followed by *response* which results in *reward* which is the *retrieve.* You don't really need the whistle at this point in order to get pup to look at you but use it anyway, preceding each cast to build up this positive association. Use a light blast now while you're this close to pup, and save the higher volume for later when he's further away from you.

We're now tossing two dummies to the same side and doing two of the same casts in succession so that pup will do it right. Remember that we're *training* pup, which consists of forming the desired habits by *repetition.*

Do not throw one to the right and one to the left and signal pup which one to get. This is great for your ego but quite confusing to the pup, and will only increase the odds for pup to make a mistake, and be corrected or threatened. This is not conducive to influencing him to like the training.

Continue using the command "FETCH" for the casts because this is the way pup was conditioned on the conditioned retrieve training table.

There are several undesirable responses which may or may not occur during the beginning of the casting drill. Pup may just sit there and do nothing in which case, you give him a "hup...hup...fetch." The "hup...hup..." being to loosen him up. Or he may want to come to you instead of going to the dummy. In this case, put him back in his sitting position, pet him a little and then step away again. Again, the "hup...hup...fetch."

Both of these improper responses are caused by confusion on the part of pup. He's just been steadied and he's worried about leaving on a retrieve from any place other than the heel position. Therefore the solution is to reassure him and jazz him up a bit. If several attempts at this don't work, then step up and pinch his ear lightly. If he's been conditioned to retrieve properly, this will get him going.

When giving pup a line, his spine should be aligned with the direction of travel.

Lesson 2: In the same manner as lesson 1, give pup 2 casts to the left, 2 to the right and 2 back. Then repeat the sequence. This total of 12 casts is enough for this lesson. Remember in addition to teaching pup to do this drill, we also want him to like it. Therefore less is better.

Lesson 3: Repeat lesson 2 lengthening the casts some according to how well pup is doing.

Lesson 4: Repeat lesson 3.

Lesson 5: Repeat lesson 3.

Lesson 6: Pup should be in the groove now on the casting drill. If he is performing the lessons confidently and liking it, you should start preceding each casting drill session with an obedience session. Your obedience drill should consist of 8 or 10 repetitions of the following:

(1) Sit Pup

(2) Walk 30 or 40 yards away

(3) Call pup to you

(4) Sit pup once or twice with a whistle blast on each of his trips to you. Then proceed with your casting drill, and repeat lesson 3.

Lesson 7: Pup should now be doing casts to the maximum length that you can throw a dummy. Repeat lesson 5. You should still be working in cover such that pup can see the white training dummies.

Lesson 8: Repeat lesson 7. Then do an obedience drill. Sit pup, walk off forty yards and then call him to you. Stop him when he's 1/2 way to you with a sit whistle. Repeat several times.

Lesson 9: Do several obedience drills. Then repeat lesson 7.

Lesson 10: Do several obedience drills. Then repeat lesson 7.

"Over" cast to the right with a step.

The "back" cast.

"Over" cast to the left with a step.

These three casts should be separate and distinct with respect to the way you give them. Start them at the belt buckle, and on the back cast stretch that arm way up so pup can see it.

Crowena

1st place
Trial Blue Ribbon
5 Championship points

Now we are going to expand this casting drill and start putting the building blocks together to get pup running a handling pattern. First you need a training area with very light cover, as again we want the dummies to be visible to pup. It needs to be of such size that the handling pattern shown will fit. We'll use this same pattern for quite a while and want to keep everything in the same place so you might wish to put stakes or markers at the various points to permanently locate them. (See illustration A).

ILLUSTRATION A

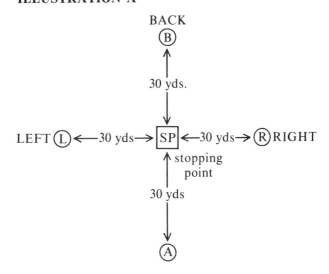

If your training area needs mowing, then you can either mow the whole thing or only those paths from "left to right" and from point A to "Back" such as illustration B.

ILLUSTRATION B

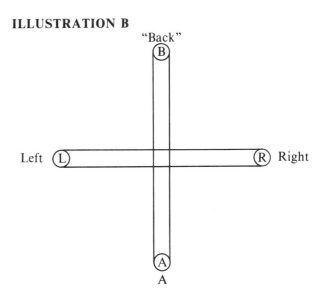

Actually, I've found that mowed paths don't seem to have much effect on teaching pup the handling pattern. The main point here is that the dummies be white and visible lying on the ground. However, if you have to mow it so that the dummies will be visible, then mowing to clear the paths will save a lot of work.

As for dimensions, those depicted in illustration A are nice but not necessary. If you need to shorten them a bit to fit your piece of ground, that's fine. I wouldn't however increase them greatly. You're trying to teach pup to respond to hand signals and to like them, not to turn him into a marathon runner. If the pattern is of reasonable dimensions then you can get more repetitions of the behavioral sequence per session without overheating and overexerting pup. If you feel a compulsion to have pup doing 100 yard over-casts then wait until later, after he's firmly grounded in the basics.

First, let me explain this pattern and the behavior we wish to achieve. The points designated as "left," "right," and "back" are piles of dummies while "A" is the point from which you, the handler, are sending pup. What we want to achieve is to have you, standing at point A, sending pup on a line toward point B. When pup reaches the stopping point you should be able to blow a single whistle blast, and have pup stop, sit, and look to you for direction. At this point you should be able to cast him right, left, or back as you so desire. When you don't blow the whistle he should continue through the stopping point to the "Back" pile of dummies.

This last concept deserves mention. If pup stops and looks to you for direction without being signaled to do so by the whistle, this is termed "popping" by the field trial contingent and is greatly frowned upon. However, for the

Do some of your casting drills on water.

"INTENSITY"
BLACK LABRADOR
Male ~ 4 yrs. old.

shooting dog, I consider it a favorable habit, plus I think it tends to manifest itself in the more intelligent and more tractable dogs. The pup who starts looking for help on blinds is going an extra step in cooperating with the handler. Additionally, stopping on the whistle is one of the most difficult of the behaviors to maintain. The "popping" pup is going to maintain the whistle stopping behavior longer, with less maintenance training, and is going to retain it better during the excitement and distractions of hunting conditions.

However, that's enough on "popping" for now. I'll discuss at the proper point how to discourage it for you field trial hopefuls.

Now that you know what the end product should be on this pattern, let's get on to building it.

Lesson 11: Take pup and walk him to the stopping point. Don't stop there. Keep walking toward the "Back" point, (B), until you're close enough to toss 6 dummies there in a pile. Then walk pup back to a point halfway between SP and B. Sit pup there and continue to SP. Give pup a whistle blast, and back cast to B. Repeat; next bring pup to a point halfway between SP and A. Line him to B, twice. Then sit him halfway between SP and R and toss two dummies to R. Give him 2 right casts each preceded by whistle blast. Then do the same to the left. To finish go to point A and line him to point B twice. If he tries to veer off toward L or R call him back, move closer to B and line him again.

In simpler terms what you've done has been:
(1) Given pup 2 shortened back casts to point B.
(2) Lined pup down the middle twice.
(3) Given pup 2 shortened right casts to R.
(4) Given pup 2 shortened left casts to L.
(5) Lined pup down the middle to "B" twice.

All casts have been preceded by the sit whistle.

Lesson 12: Take pup and walk close enough to the Back position to toss 7 dummies there. Then sit pup on the stopping point and, leaving him there, walk part way to point A. Give him a whistle blast and back cast to point B. Repeat this. Next go to point A and line pup twice to point B. Then put pup on the stopping point while you walk over and toss two dummies to point R. You go back to a point halfway between A and SP and give him two right casts to point R. Repeat this in the same manner for two left casts to handler standing half way between A and SP. With the handler in same spot line pup to B. Then the handler backs up to A and again lines pup to B.

The simplified translation of the above is:
(1) Give pup 2 back casts to point B.
(2) Line him twice down the middle.
(3) Give him two Right casts to R.
(4) Give him two Left casts to L.
(5) Give him one back cast.
(6) Line him once down the middle.

Lesson 13: Repeat lesson 12.

Lesson 14: Do several obedience drills and then repeat lesson 12.

Lesson 15: Do several obedience drills and then repeat lesson 12.

Lesson 16: Do several obedience drills and then repeat lesson 12.

Lesson 17: Now we're to the point of trying all this together. Put pup on the stopping point and let him watch as you put out the dummies. Walk over and toss 6 dummies on point B. Then return to a point halfway between A and the stopping point where pup is sitting. Give him a back cast. Next attach a 50 ft rope to pup's collar. Since you are located halfway between A and the stopping point and are thus 15 yds (45 ft) from the stopping point, this rope will be your insurance if pup fails to respond to your sit whistle. Give pup a line and send him toward B. Retain one end of the rope in your hand. As he approaches (10 ft. from) the stopping point give him an energetic sit whistle, followed immediately by a barked command "HERE." He'll either stop and look at you or hit the end of the rope. In either case get him sitting with a whistle blast or verbal command. You may have to walk a few steps closer to him. As soon as he sits give him some verbal "good dogs," (but don't let him get up from his sit.). Then give him a back cast.

This verbal encouragement is to loosen pup up. The first few times you stop him on the whistle, he may be a bit worried and not want to go when you give him the cast. If you give him the prior verbal encouragement and he still freezes, try "hup...hup" and then the cast. That should break him loose. If it doesn't you may need to walk over to him and administer an ear pinch or two; then back away and try the cast again.

Next repeat this sequence of:

(1) Sending him down the middle.
(2) Stopping and sitting him at stopping point.
(3) Giving back cast to dummy at B.

Now, to set pup's brain for the next stop and cast sequence, walk him over to the stopping point and leave him sitting there to watch while you toss two dummies to point R. Walk back to A, give him the whistle blast and cast to R. Next, with you at the halfway point and with the end of insurance rope in hand, line pup down the middle and stop and sit him at the stopping point. Then give him a right case with the command "FETCH."

This same sequence should be repeated for two left casts. After that, line him down the middle with a stop at the stopping point and back cast to B. Then line him down the middle without a stop. This concludes the lesson.

There are two points worthy of note here. You are working pup from a point (halfway between A and stopping point) close to the stopping point because the closer you are to pup when you blow the sit whistle, the more likely he is to stop. Of course, your 50 ft insurance rope also has some influence on the distance from stopping point. The other

Stump Blind (cypress)
Reelfoot Lake, Tennessee
for Diver Hunting

thing you're doing is giving pup a programming cast just prior to the full sequence of line, stop-on-whistle, cast. This programming cast is the one which leaves pup sitting on the stopping point while he watches you toss two dummies to the appropriate spot. Thus they are fresh on his mind when you walk back to the halfway point (between A and stopping point) and give him the programming cast. This sets the stage so that you've increased the odds for a successful performance of the full sequence of line, stop-on-whistle, and cast.

Again, I emphasize the value of the short lesson here. The above is plenty taxing for pup's brain. Do the steps described and no more. You'd like this to be more game than grind.

Lesson 18: Repeat lesson 17.

Lesson 19: Repeat lesson 17.

Lesson 20: Repeat lesson 17.

Lesson 21: Repeat lesson 17.

Lesson 22: Now we're ready to try this handling pattern in final form. Taking pup with you toss two dummies at point R. Then two at point L. Last, go over and toss 4 to point B. You do it in that order so that the dummies at point B, being the last down, will be the freshest and most tempting in pup's mind. This is to counteract a tendency some pups will have to go forward R or L when you're lining them to B. They do this because the line B crosses the stopping point and is therefore not as much fun as line R or L would be. So, for a while, follow the prescribed order of putting out dummies.

After the dummies are out, begin by lining pup from A to B without a stop. Then on the next 6 runs stop him at the stopping point and give him 2 left casts, 2 right casts, and two back casts in whatever order you desire. Then finish with a line down the middle without a stop.

About now, pup is going to start making some mistakes on casts and there are two things that you can do to improve his performance. First, when he goes the wrong way on a cast (if you give left cast and he goes back), stop him immediately with a sit whistle. If you stop him when he's gone only three steps in the wrong direction, you'll change his mind much more easily than if you let him go twenty steps in the wrong direction. Second, when you do stop him quickly and he still wants to go the wrong way, then stop him again and call him back toward you 10 or 20 feet. Then sit him and try the cast again. This act of bringing pup toward you (with whistle signal or command "HERE") seems to erase his preconceived notion and he'll nearly always give you the proper response.

Lesson 23: Repeat lesson 22.

Lesson 24: Repeat lesson 22.

Lesson 25: Repeat lesson 22.

Lesson 26: Here's where I like to throw a little change. Up to now you've been giving pup his casts with a visual cue and a verbal command; "back" for back and "fetch" for right and left.

Canada Goose ~
crowe wa

Traditionally retrievers are trained to cast right or left with a hand signal to the appropriate direction and the verbal command "OVER." I suggest that this can be improved upon for the hunting dog.

If pup is dependent on a visual signal for direction when he is out a hundred yards from the duck blind, he may have a bit of trouble. In contrast to the field trialer in his white handling jacket, the average duck hunter goes to great effort and expense to make himself invisible. It would seem, therefore, a bit foolish to train pup to respond to visual signals on blind retrieves. The further pup gets from the duck blind, the tougher it will be for him to follow your camouflaged signals.

The solution is a sound cue for direction. This would be either a verbal or whistle command for each direction of travel. The simplest cue would be "left" for left, "right" for right and "back" for back. The handler won't be likely to get confused and pup won't be so dependant on a visual cue from a camouflaged hunter.

At this point in the program pup should be running the pattern confidently with relatively few mistakes. Now is the time to change your verbal cue from "fetch" to "right" and "left." Keep giving the visual hand signals, however, as it will take quite a while for pup to transform from the visual to the verbal cue.

So, for this lesson do the same as you did in lesson 25 but change the verbal cues for the over casts from "fetch" to "right" and "left."

Lesson 27: Repeat lesson 26.
Lesson 28: Repeat lesson 26.
Lesson 29: Repeat lesson 26.
Lesson 30: Repeat lesson 26.

Pup should be fairly good on the pattern now. Keep running it. You want these habits super conditioned. The more you run pup on the handling pattern the stronger the habits will become and the better he'll perform in the excitement of hunting conditions.

Antique
Short Bird
Decoy 1983

Pup should have twenty or more pattern lessons over the next month before you start running him on blind retrieves and then the blinds should be fairly short. You want pup to develop a belief in you on blinds. Therefore he should always be successful. In keeping with this you should exercise some selectivity on what you send him for on a blind during his initial season of hunting. Make sure you know there is a bird there, and where it is. Hunting buddies are sometimes a bit erroneous in marking the fall of a bird they think they hit.

Remember, the hand signals are trained behavior and as such require periodic maintenance conditioning to stay sharp. Always return to running the handling pattern. This is where the proper habits are maintained and conditioned. You can and should, as pup's proficiency increases, change the location and dimensions of the pattern, but keep running it. That's what will keep pup running good blind retrieves.

"KEEP ON GOING" DRILL

The drills pup has mastered so far will provide sufficient skills to meet the needs of most hunting situations. If you want to develop his lining talents further, there are a couple of other drills that I recommend.

The first drill is the "keep-on-going" drill and can be tackled as soon as pup is steady and has been through the basic sight blind drills and handling pattern. During pup's initial training program this drill will increase his lining proficiency. As he gains age and hunting experience, it will be quite valuable in counteracting the "30 yard hunt" syndrome.

This "thirty yard hunt" syndrome is a habit which builds into the hunting dog who gets no maintenance training between hunting seasons. It's also more prevalent in dogs belonging to hunters who are good with the shotgun. Most of the birds this dog picks up fall within a distance of approximately 30 yards. Therefore, Fido tends more and more to hunt at thirty yards. He gets out that far, puts down his nose, and becomes a canine vacuum cleaner. He starts failing on that occasional wing-tipped bird that sails 100 yards.

Some between season maintenance training will help counteract this. When you can get a helper, send him out in the field to throw long marks. When you can't, do the "keep-on-going" drill. Here it is:

Find a field with very light or no cover such that pup can see the white training dummies lying on the ground. Put out six or eight in a line spaced about 15 to 20 yards apart as shown in figure 1, where A is the point from which you and pup are running and X's represent dummies.

A   X   X   X   X   X   X

|←——30 yds.——→|←15 yds→|

Line pup successively to the dummies. You may have a little trouble at first getting him to go past where he picked up the last one. This is normal because we have been programming him by repetition to expect to find another dummy in the same place. This drill will also help to counteract that programming.

Green Wing Teal
The Jet fighter of the sky —

TRIPLE LINE DRILL

The next drill, the triple line, will refine both your and pup's skill in taking a line in a particular direction. This drill also will help counterbalance that tendency of pup's to go back to the last spot where he picked up a dummy.

For this one you'll need a fairly large field, again preferably with light cover. You'll use this same field and same relative positions for a number of sessions so you may want to stake the location to insure that they remain constant.

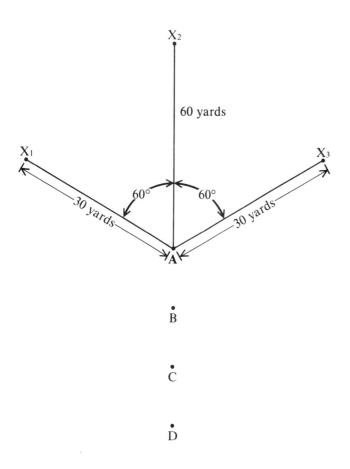

Lesson 1: Working pup from Point A, do two repetitions of a sight blind planted at X_1.

Lesson 2: Working pup from Point A, do two repetitions of a sight blind to Point X_2.

Lesson 3: Working pup from Point A, do two repetitions of a sight blind to Point X_3.

Lesson 4: Working pup from Point A, do two sight blinds each to X_1, X_2, and X_3. Vary the order in which pup does them. If pup takes off for the wrong one (one other than that toward which you're lining him) either stop him

with the whistle and cast him back to the proper line or call him back and start over. Use whichever works better.

When pup is consistently taking the indicated line from you working from Point A, move back 10 yds to Point B and work from there. When he's error free there, move back another 10 yards to Point C. You can continue progressively backing up in this manner until the angular separation between lines is about 10 degrees. The dog/handler team which can line within 10 degrees of the desired azimuth is a well-trained team and is more than adequate for any hunting situation.

Two cautions are in order for this drill. As you back up pup will be doing a lot of running in a short period of time. Don't turn it into an endurance contest. Two or three repetitions on each of the three sight blinds is plenty for one session. If pup's getting winded, give him a pause or two during the lesson to catch his breath. During hot humid weather, be especially careful. You're just standing there while pup does all the work, so he can overheat before you realize it.

Bull Pintail
at Rest

Typical Bayou Guide (cajun caller, hip boots, push pole)

The Pirogue—The Louisana Duck Boat—They say the good ones will float in a heavy dew—

Chapter 9
Water Training

Cold water is the place where pup needs all the go power he can get. When it's zero degrees with a 15 knot wind and you've just knocked down a couple of long ducks, you'll find out whether you've got a dog who loves water, or, more aptly, a dog who loves retrieving ducks and has minimum inhibitions about piling into the water.

Minimum inhibition is the name of the game on water training. You want pup to develop through his training program an affinity for water, not an aversion. It's no accident that this chapter on water training is tacked on after the meat of the training program. We want all the control work, steadying, and conditioning of responses to occur on land work. Water should be pup's dessert, a place of great fun, many ducks, and success. Build the control habits on land and then go to water with only the chore of building in pup the confidence that there is always a duck out there in the water to retrieve.

This is not to say that you should let him be a wild Indian around water or deprive him of water work completely, but that the control should be required on water only after it's thoroughly conditioned on land. If he's not quite reliable on steadiness, keep a hand on that check cord when you're doing water work. Try not to get in a situation where you have to correct him on the water.

Pup's water work should progress parallel to his control program but separate from it. He should have been introduced to the water as a puppy and should have gotten plenty of successful water retrieves prior to starting the obedience training. A good variation in the obedience program is to give him the happy dummies in the water and then move over 20 or 30 yards on land for an obedience lesson, finishing with more happy dummies in the water.

When you're in the conditioned retrieve training portion it's best to stay away from retrieving on both land and water.

As previously mentioned, during the steadying phase by all means include water work, but do it with pup wearing a short (2 or 3 ft.) check chord, holding him so that you won't have to correct him for breaking on the water.

Pup's water marks should start out easy and get progressively harder as his proficiency improves. You want him always to be successful. This applies to double retrieves also. Always give him a single first for the memory bird, and then repeat it with the second bird added. Start them short where pup can see them floating on the water and then gradually increase the distance.

One factor on the water which can increase the complexity of retrieves is bank running. This is pup's tendency to take the driest route rather than the most direct route to the bird. Pup does this not because he's avoiding the water but because he can get there faster by land. The simplest way to counteract this bank running tendency is to keep pup out of tempting situations especially during his early training. If his water retrieves are set up such that there aren't tempting places available to run along the bank he won't develop this habit, and consequently will be less prone to run the bank later when tempting situations do appear. Throw his dummies or birds where they are much closer by water than by land. Don't test him; set it up so that he won't be tempted. One of the most important factors will be how far back from the water pup is when sent on the retrieve. The further back he is, the more prone he'll be to look for a quicker land route. So all his early water work should be done right at the edge of the water. More on bank running will follow later in this chapter.

Goose Band-
Hovey Lake-1976
15 lb.
Greater Canadian
9 Years Old

Sight Blinds in water

After pup is steady, doing water doubles proficiently, and performing well on land sight blinds, start sight blinds in the water. You'll have to change your procedure a bit as no one has walked on water in quite a while.

Happy dummies in the water. Rev-up pup by sending him fast.

This is the way you like to see them get into the water.

Pup is obedient, steady, conditioned on the retrieve, and confident in the water.

That checkcord he's trailing isn't for steadiness.

Lesson 1: First find yourself a small pond, such as the one illustrated. Sit pup at point A, and, leaving him there to watch, walk around the bank and toss out dummies in a line as indicated by the X's. Use white training dummies so pup

can see them lying in the water. Walk back to pup at point A and successively line him to pick up the dummies. Note that you're working pup from the edge of the water to decrease his temptation to run around the bank. Also note that the furthest dummies are no closer than 15 or 20 feet to the far bank. This is to decrease the temptation for pup to return via the bank.

Another factor which will tend to keep pup in the water is his tendency to repeat the same path he took the first time. The first retrieve for the closest dummy will establish his path and entry point for the subsequent retrieves.

If pup, after grabbing the first dummy, wants to veer toward the bank to get out early give him a sharp command "HERE" and take several emphatic steps in the direction you need to move him to keep him in the water. The conditioned retrieve training should have conditioned him sufficiently to respond to your body movement. If this doesn't work, just shorten the retrieve to the point that pup is below the threshold of temptation for the wrong bank. Then progressively lengthen the retrieves in small enough increments that you don't exceed that threshold.

You'd like pup to go and come by water in this exercise because we're going to convert this sight blind drill to a water handling pattern later. Going and coming by water will make the water handling pattern easier for pup to grasp.

Lesson 2: Come back to the same pond the next day. Again leave pup at point A, where he can watch as you walk around and toss 3 dummies to the positions shown. Walk

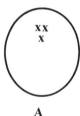

back to A, which would be the same place for each lesson, and line pup successively to the dummies. I know this lesson seems short, but it is supposed to be. You want pup's enthusiasm up and you don't want to clutter his memory and navigation system with other locations of dummies for this particular pond.

Lesson 3: Repeat lesson 2.

Lesson 4: Repeat lesson 2.

Lesson 5: Pup should now be lining across the pond with enthusiasm and purpose. If he is, you can dispense with letting him watch while you toss out the dummies. Leave him out of sight while you put out the dummies, and you'll now be sending him on semi-blinds in the water.

Lesson 6: Repeat lesson 5.

Sight blinds in the water. . .

. . . build confidence and enthusiam.

Maintain the requirement for pup to sit and deliver to hand as a reminder to pup that the enthusiasm is controlled.

Checkcord is further insurance for this bank running situation.

Presto! The magic rope kept him off the bank. (The other end is in the trainer's hand.)

Water Handling Pattern

Now you can expand this water lining drill into a handling pattern. Keep working on the same pond and using the same locations for handler, dog, and dummies. The big item here will be stopping on the whistle. Pup needs to be well educated on the land handling pattern before trying it in the water. He should be running the land handling pattern like a clock; then go to water. If pup is not doing this then keep to the land handling pattern and just lining in the water until his responses are consistent enough that you're pretty sure he'll stop on the whistle in the water.

Lesson 7: Here's where you convert to the water handling pattern. Go back to the same pond and, with pup out of sight, put out your dummies as illustrated. Put white

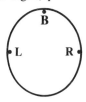

dummies at B. You can put them on the shoreline now as pup's habits will be strong enough that he won't return by land. Put orange dummies at L and R and insure that the distance is such that you can throw a dummy from A and hit fairly close to L or R. Put two orange dummies on the shoreline at L and similarly two at R. The reason for the orange is that pup has very poor color vision and the orange is much harder for him to see. Thus we'll have an easier time of it keeping his initial line toward A.

101

Success! Pup has made the retrieves properly, going and coming by water. He had no opportunity to do otherwise.

Line pup across to B once. Then line him again and when he's abreast of L give him a stop whistle, followed immediately if needed, by the emphatic command "HERE." As soon as pup has turned and looked at you give him an emphatic hand signal with the command "BACK" to cast him to B. Then repeat this sequence. Next send him; stop him abreast of L and when he's looking at you give him an emphatic hand signal with a large step or two and the command "LEFT." If he doesn't take the cast, try again with hand signal and the command "FETCH." If this doesn't do it, while he's turned and looking at you throw a dummy to L. Then try the cast again. He'll respond properly with the thrown dummy. Next repeat the sequence for L and do two casts in the same manner to R. Finish with two "BACK" casts to B.

You're sending him down the middle more often to counteract any tendency on pup's part to line toward L or R which would deprive him of the behavioral sequence of stopping on the whistle and taking a cast. As on the land pattern, when pup goes the wrong way on a cast, the quicker you stop him and repeat the cast, the better the odds of changing his mind.

In summary, in this lesson you:
    (1) lined him down the middle to B.
    (2) twice lined him, stopping him abreast of L, and cast him to B.
    (3) twice lined, stopped and cast to L.
    (4) twice lined, stopped and cast to R.
    (4) twice lined, stopped and cast to B.

This sequence will probably get pup popping, which I consider desirable in a hunting dog. If you don't want the

Pup's a little reluctant on his water entry.

Here's a rig that gently but inevitably gets him in while keeping the trainer dry.

popping then greatly increase the proportion of times you line him down the middle to B without stopping him on the whistle.

Lesson 8: Repeat lesson 7.

Lesson 9: Repeat lesson 7.

Lesson 10: Repeat lesson 7.

Pup should now be fairly proficient on this water handling pattern. You should come back periodically and run this drill to strengthen his water handling skills. The frequency should be determined by the quality of his performance. As with the land handling pattern, the more often he repeats it the better he'll get on blind retrieves.

INTRODUCTIONS TO DECOYS, BOATS, ETC.

At some point in pup's education, he should be introduced to some of your duck hunting accessories. During the steadying process is a good time for the duck call. Throw him a couple of shackled ducks and after they are down, blow on your duck call a bit before sending pup to retrieve.

Introduce pup to decoys after he's conditioned on the retrieve and retrieving confidently in the water. The method I prefer involved using a helper to throw shackled ducks for pup to retrieve. Put the decoys out anchored individually in a typical hunting set up, and place your helper either down the bank or out in a boat positioned so he can throw the ducks to land fifteen or twenty yards out past the decoys. The object here is to teach pup that there is nothing interesting about decoys except that there are ducks to be found out past them. Have your helper shoot in the air and throw a duck. If, while heading for the duck, pup gets too distracted by the decoys or picks up a decoy, simply have the helper shoot again and throw another duck closer to pup. As soon as he figures out that those fat tempting ducks are to be had out past the decoys he'll lose interest in the plastic imitations. Thus there's no need to correct him for picking up a decoy.

The other problem which may occur is for pup to be afraid of the decoys. Here you should clear a wide path through the decoys and shorten the retrieve to where the duck is falling in his path. Jazz pup up, and send him fast. Then progressively lengthen the retrieves until he's going through and past the decoys. As he gains confidence, gradually narrow the path until you have a normal spread of decoys again. Over a period of two weeks, four or five lessons of five or six retrieves each, should be sufficient to head off any future problems with decoys.

Another introduction, which ties in nicely with the decoys, is the boat. After pup is retrieving confidently through the decoys, work him from a boat which is pulled firmly up on the bank so that it is quite stable.

If you do much hunting from a boat there is a beneficial extra which can be introduced at this point in pup's boat training. This is to train pup to shake at sufficient distance from you to keep you dry. The key factor here is that most pups who have been through conditioned retrieve training will not shake until you've taken the duck from them. To utilize this trait you simply place pup a good long arm's length from yourself. Then sit him, reach way over and take the duck. Pup will stand up to shake and you can then sit him again. You will be a good long arm's length away and stay dry.

Start this drill with the boat pulled up on the bank and stable. As pup enters the boat grasp his collar and physically put him in the desired place. Accompany this action with a specific command. "PUP KENNEL" or the command used to put him in his pen is a good one and one that will facilitate the association process. When he's sitting in his place return

This must come after the conditioned retrieve or pup may not grab the dummy after you get him there.

Introduction to decoys. Leave a "slot" through the middle of the spread.

Introduction to boat should begin with boat pulled well up on bank where it is a stable platform.

When pup enters the boat with duck, always direct him to his proper place.

Sit him and then reach over to take the duck. Then let him shake.

When you move to deeper water pup will need some assistance entering the boat.

After he's in, send him to his place, sit him, and then reach over and take duck.

Then let him shake. This will keep you dry (which helps a lot on those cold days).

to yours. Reach out and take the duck, allow him to shake, and then sit him back down. When pup has been through sufficient repetitions of this to make him go to his place on the verbal comand, you're ready to gradually move the boat to deeper water. Pup is sufficiently trained when he exits and enters the boat confidently in swimming water.

You'll have to assist pup in entering the boat in swimming water. Depending on the type of boat this can usually be accomplished by pushing on the back of pup's neck after his forequarters are over the gunwale. This push will give him the purchase to heave his hindquarters in. Some boat designs require a hefty pull on the collar from you to get him in. In either case, practice the assisted boat entry in deep water, after he's comfortable in entry and exit in shallow water. You don't want to teach him to associate unpleasantness with a boat.

WATER PROBLEMS

Water problems with pup can generally be traced back to one of two causes. They are usually either a lack of control or a lack of enthusiasm for the water retrieve. Lets look at the most common case first; that of lack of control. This problem will manifest itself usually in one of four ways.

(1) **Pup won't come out of the water:** This is a simple lack of obedience. Pup is not responding well enough to the command "HERE." The solution is to cease the water work. Continue land work with heavy emphasis on obedience

108

drills and conditioning the dog to the command "HERE." Sometimes it is also helpful to stay away from the water until you've completed the conditioned retrieve training. Much of the "not-coming" behavior derives from the play pup associated with retrieving. The conditioned retrieve training reduces the play association and reinforces the work aspect of retrieving, thus it is often valuable in reducing this "not-coming" behavior.

If you've got a real outlaw get out the 100 foot check cord. Use a polypropylene check cord which floats, to lessen the risk of entanglement. Keep all the retrieves 100 feet or less in distance so that you can always have check cord in hand. When pup is reliable about coming you can start shortening the check cord and lengthening the retrieves. First go to a 75 ft. check cord. Throw the duck out 100 ft., and send pup. If you've done the groundwork properly and pup is reliable he's not going to realize you're not holding on to the end of it. In like manner you progress to a 10 ft. check cord which you should let pup continue to wear until you are certain that he won't revert to his former undesirable behavior.

(2) **Pup drops the duck in the water on his return and won't pick it back up:** This is usually a result of deficiences in two areas. First, pup is not coming to you well enough. If he's responding well to the command "HERE" he won't have time to drop the duck. Second, pup isn't conditioned retrieve trained properly. If he were, you would give the command fetch when he dropped the duck. This would cause him to pick it back up, and the command "HERE" would bring him on in to you. The solution is to cease the water work while you reprogram the deficient responses on land. The reason for ceasing the water work is that by indulging in undesirable behavior pup is strengthening it. Remember that he learns by habit formation which is a function of repetition.

The exception to this is the pup who exhibits this duck dropping behavior only with ducks. If he's OK on dummies then continue his water work with dummies. Thus you are strengthening desirable behavior. Concurrently you can be reinforcing the deficient responses in the land segment of his program. Try this for a couple of weeks before going back to ducks.

(3) **Pup won't pick up a duck:** This is almost always a result of improper introduction to ducks. A big quacking, flapping, pecking (training ducks get quite mean and aggressive about pecking pup) mallard is hardly the initial contact you want pup to have with ducks. Start him on dead pigeons, then go to a wing clipped pigeon. When he's comfortable and aggressive with these, go to a dead duck and then progress to a live duck with wings taped to body, feet taped together, and bill taped in closed position.

Another factor to consider in his duck introduction in the water is pup's degree of self confidence in the water. If it's his third water retrieve and he's not yet even comfortable

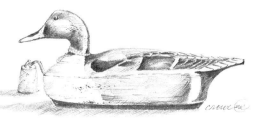

Old Pintail Decoy—
Hand Made—Maker
and Date Unknown—

This four-month old pup obviously doesn't swim properly.

about being in the water he may not be inclined to take on that duck. Don't forget to look at it from pup's perspective. He's down in the water and on eye level with the duck. On the other hand, if it's his fiftieth water retrieve and he's quite confident and aggressive and has had lots of dead ducks in the water, he'll be much more prone to tackle that live duck looking him in the eye.

The above cases should give you the general idea on control problems in the water. They are usually a result of trying to do too much too soon. Develop consistent responses on land, and when pup is reliable, require them in the water.

The other big water bugaboo is lack of go power. Pup is not aggressive in the water. He's not developing the go power he'll need to sustain him when that water gets really cold. The main rule here is that if you can't solve it with birds, you'd better get another pup.

Looking at it more closely, let's consider the pup who won't go in the water at all. He's either never been in or has bad associations with the water. The solution here is a bathing suit for you. Go in the water yourself; coax pup in. Pull him in gently to you with a rope. Pet him profusely when he get to you. When he's comfortable in the water get him revved up with lot's of short fast retrieves using live birds. The main point here is no horror shows. You want pup to like the water so be careful not to scare him.

Another solution is to let pup out with another dog who likes the water. Throw a few retrieves for the water dog.

The lightweight canvas dummy doesn't help much.

The large plastic "knobby" dummy is heavier and gets his front end down in the water for proper swimming.

Pup will frequently respond to this competitive situation by bailing into the water. Don't carry this on too long, however. As soon as pup has been in a few times, put the other dog up and give pup a couple of very short retrieves in the water. Otherwise, if the other dog always gets the dummy, pup may get discouraged and quit trying.

When pup gets going in the water but has trouble learning to swim properly there is something you can do to speed up the process. If he's swimming with his head up high and front paws slapping at the water, go to a large plastic dummy for him to retrieve. The extra weight will tend to pull his front end down into the water where it should be for efficient swimming.

What about the pup who goes slowly into the water? This can sometimes be the result of control problems and consequent nagging and over correction. If every time pup is around the water he gets nagged and corrected, he'll likely develop a poor picture of water and lose enthusiasm. The solution here is to get the control responses properly conditioned on land first and then go to water. Additionally, give pup lots of clipped wing pigeons and shackled ducks in the water. This should get him revved up. If it doesn't there may be some doubt as to how well he'll perform when the weather gets cold and the going gets tough.

This brings us to another cause for lack of enthusiasm in the water, and that is putting pup too young in cold water. A young pup sometimes lacks the toughness and physical protection of a mature coat of hair. I don't like to put pups in severely cold hunting conditions until they are eighteen months old. The same is true for winter water training; one should use birds instead of dummies and make the retrieves shorter than for warm water.

The last case we'll look at is the pup who is charging aggressively into the water but lacks the persistence to succeed on longer or more difficult retrieves. This is usually another case of trying too much too soon. Pup has not had enough easier water retrieves to develop the confidence that the duck is where his eyes saw it fall. The more successful water retrieves pup performs the greater will be his confidence. Obviously, for the pup who lacks persistence, the progression from simple water retrieves to the more difficult has been too rapid. The solution is to shorten and simplify followed by a more gradual progression to the more difficult retrieves. Here again lots of birds, i.e. shackled ducks, make for a more rapid and more dramatic improvement.

Ideally we'd like pup to think of water as the place where he always finds lots of scrumptious, exciting ducks. This sort of programming produces a duck dog for whom no water is too cold and no retrieve too long.

BANK RUNNING

In keeping with our primary rule of consistency you should decide early on in pup's water program whether you will allow bank running or not allow it. If you're going to allow it then decide how much to allow.

For the uninitiated let me describe bank running in a bit more detail. There are several ways to do it. In the illustrated situation you and pup are at point A. The duck is

at point X. There are 3 ways pup can go to retrieve that duck. (1) He can pile into the water on a direct line to X, grab the duck and return straight on the reverse of his outgoing line; (2) He can pile into the water and take a direct line to the duck, grab it, and then hit the bank on the far side and return by land; (3) He can run around on the bank to the far side, hop in the water, grab the duck, get back out on the far side and return by land. That should define bank running.

What you as the trainer must decide early on is how much to allow; then be consistent in your demands during pup's training program. This is largely a matter of personal preference.

For a hunting dog there is no intrinsic evil in bank running. In some cases bank running is desirable as in the case of river hunting. If you drop a duck in a fast flowing river, pup is going to be much more successful if he runs down the bank to a point abreast of or down stream of the duck before jumping into the water for the retrieve.

On the other hand, it is esthetically very pleasing to have a pup who piles into the water on a straight line to the bird. So for the average hunter, I think the solution is a compromise. Program pup in his early water work for staying in the water and past that don't worry about it.

By programming, I mean always set up the retrieve so that pup will go and come by water. As mentioned previously, the main factors are how far back from the bank you are running pup and where the dummy is being thrown

Figure 1

Figure 2

relative to the bank. Looking at figure 1 to illustrate, if you are running pup from point A with the dummy falling at X then he is probably going to run around the bank. Conversely, looking at figure 2, pup will probably not run the bank in this situation.

Pup should be kept out of bank running situations in his early water work by proper engineering of the retrieves. Included in this is always throwing the dummies or birds out in the water rather than on the bank. If pup never finds birds or dummies on the bank, the bank will have less attraction for him.

Timber Mallard Droppin In —

For those with field trial aspirations the bank training must be carried a good bit further. Field trial water tests are generally engineered so that the bank runner will fail. Therefore, quite a bit more bank training is required. Along with popping I feel that bank running is greatly overemphasized as a fault in field trial performance. However, if you plan to compete in field trials you better do the bank training. This training should be delayed until pup has gotten through conditioned retrieve training, steadying, and, preferably, handling on a pattern. These will give you the added tools and channels of communication to get across to pup the proper route to and from the bird when tempting banks are in his path.

Since this is a program for training hunting dogs, I'll not go into great detail on bank training but I will go through an example or two of training lessons. These examples will apply to the pup who has never been put in situations to allow him to run the bank. Pups who have developed the habit may require somewhat sterner methods. Again, pup should also have had enough water work that he's doing simple doubles confidently.

Here are two bank training situations and how to conduct them. What they do is teach pup what is expected. Variations of these lessons should be taught until pup has a good behavior base. Then you can correct deviations from this desired behavior.

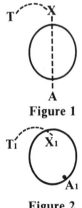

Figure 1

Figure 2

Situation 1

Figure 1 represents a small pond through which you'd like pup to go to retrieve the dummy X, thrown by thrower T. Pup and handler are working from point A. To teach this, what we'll do is use pup's tendency to repeat a previously traveled path. We'll break the path down to several components, teach these, and then put them together. First, as in figure 2, move pup up to the waters edge at A_1. Pull the thrower in to T_1 where he can toss dummy to X_1 which is in the water 5 or 10 feet from the bank.

Step 1: The handler at A_1 tosses pup a dummy 10 ft. out in the water to show pup where to enter the water. Send pup on retrieve.

Step 2: Have thrower throw dummy to X_1. Send pup on retrieve.

Step 3: Move thrower back to point where he can throw to X as shown in figure 1. Still working from point A_1 of figure 2 send pup on the retrieve. When he gets to the far bank he'll tend to hang up there because that's where he found the last dummy. Therefore as he approaches the bank have the thrower shout and throw another dummy at X of figure 1.

After pup picks up the dummy at X and begins his return you need to be alert. If he starts to veer off his line back to you, showing intent to run around, you must take

Putting on the Brakes in that North wind ~ Black Jack ~

several vigorous steps in the appropriate direction while authoritatively barking the command "HERE." If this doesn't put him back on course to return via water, walk around and meet him on the bank by which he's returning. Upon meeting him don't take the dummy. Walk him at heel back to the point where he should have entered the water. Sit pup there. Take the dummy from him and toss it out about 10 feet into the water on the return line. Leaving pup sitting in place, walk back around to point A₁ and call pup to you with the command "HERE." Try the retrieve again, omitting the extra throw as he approaches the far bank. If several repetitions of this walking around to show pup the return line don't get the idea across and pup is still trying to run around, sterner measures are in order. The next time meet him on the prohibited bank and give him several raps with the stick coupled with the command "NO." Be sure this correction occurs at the place you don't want pup to be because this is how he will associate it. Then put pup back on his proper return line, and leaving him there, walk around to A, and then summon him. As he comes back through the water give him some verbal praise and, upon delivery of the dummy, a few pets. A few repetitions of this will convince pup that the only successful route back to you is through the water.

When pup is performing properly from the A₁ point you can move back from the water to A. This may take one session or several sessions spread over as many days.

Situation 2: After pup is fairly proficient at tests similar to situation 1, you can progress to a refinement of stay-in-the water training as depicted in figure 3.

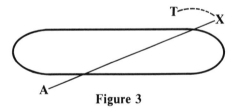

Figure 3

Here as in situation 1, the object is to teach pup to travel a straight line from his starting point A to retrieve the dummy or bird at X, and return via the same line. I'm not quite sure of the intrinsic value of this straight line, but field trial judges seem to have an affinity for cranking this basic principle into their water tests. So, if you're going field trialing, you'd better teach it. You treat this training situation the same as the earlier one. Break it down into parts. Teach the parts. Then put them together.

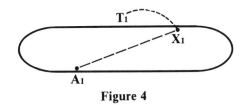

Figure 4

As shown in figure 4, working pup from point A_1; first the handler tosses the pup a short dummy to establish his water entry point. Then have thrower at T_1 toss dummy in the water. After pup completes this, move thrower back to point T of figure 3 and throw dummy to X. Attempts to return via land should be dealt with as they were in situation 1. After pup has performed properly from point A_1 move back to point A of figure 3 and have him do the complete test.

These two examples are a very simplified version of the water training required for the field trial performer. They merely illustrate principles which may be incorporated as parts of more complex water tests. They are intended to give you a brief glimpse of some of the water training necessary for the field trial pup and an indication of how to go about it. Further detail is beyond the scope of a book on training the shooting dog.

All hand-Made Wooden
Black Jack Head
for easy Transport—
1926

This pup is properly electronically trained.

Taking the
Elevator
Mallard—

Chapter 10
Electronic Training

For the duck hunter I have three words of advice on the electric collar. ***Don't use it.***

It is a fantastic training device and can be used on any dog but not by any person. The electric collar requires a skilled user because it is a *training device* not a trainer. You must be able to train a dog without the electric collar before you can train him with it. It is used to condition responses. Therefore the response must be previously trained by conventional means.

The big user problem with the electric collar is knowing and practicing when *not* to use it. That little red button is so easy to push. The skilled user knows when not to push it. The unskilled user usually pushes it when he's mad which, with some people, can be frequently.

The electric collar, or electronic training, is a wonderful tool and helps the skillful trainer turn out a beautifully trained dog. If you want yours electronically trained, send him to a qualified professional trainer for the necessary programming.

Arkansas Rice Tank
Tim Doepel / Phil Crowe 1983

Chapter 11
Introduction to Hunting

You've spent all this time and effort training pup; he is ready to go hunting, but there are still a few things which you need to keep in mind. Most important is the fact that pup is a greenhorn. He has no idea why you got in that boat in the predawn darkness and motored out to a funny little box to sit there. He also senses your excitement and is either in turn excited or perhaps confused. He needs a little help on his first few hunts to figure out what is going on. He also needs to understand that the same standards of behavior apply here, as they did in training sessions, in spite of the handler's excited state. Pup can do some strange things on that first hunt, so exercise your patience. He may become overly excited and appear to forget much of his training or he may be worried and confused. A little common sense is necessary here. The overly excited pup should be dealt with firmly while the confused one needs a bit of support.

He may in spite of your training pick up a decoy or two instead of the first duck. Don't get excited about it. He's merely confused. When he's seen a few ducks, at the instant of impact, fold and hit the water, everything will begin to fall into place. He'll know what you're there for. When he's seen a few get hit, then he'll begin to understand where these falling ducks come from and he'll begin scanning the skies for them.

You'd like pup to figure out what is going on as quickly as possible, and there are several things you can do to promote this.

If you're planning cold weather hunting for ducks or geese in ice, snow or chilly winds, it might be a good idea to hold off taking pup until he's around 18 months old. He needs to be physically tough and have an adult coat of hair before he faces those tough conditions for his first hunt. For cold weather hunting any dog, young or old, needs to be in good condition and have plenty of weight. Muscle mass and a layer of fat will help keep him warm. Let him learn how much fun hunting is before he gets into the rough stuff.

Now for pup's introductory duck hunt. First, keep him under control. You don't want to waste all of that time spent training him on obedience in the yard by teaching him that it doesn't apply in a hunting situation.

Take him from the car at heel and have him sit and stay while you get your gear together. Then release him for a couple of minutes to clean out. It's back at heel for the journey to the boat or blind. If he's too excited to remember his training, keep a lead on him.

While I'm on the subject of taking pup out of the car, it is a good idea to *always* take him out under control. Keep him under control until you are ready to release him and it is safe to do so. He doesn't need to run wild for fifteen minutes to burn off energy. If you allow him to run free, you're training him to be disobedient upon leaving the car. This also applies to the house or kennel. This practice of letting pup run wild for 10 minutes after coming out of car or kennel merely trains in a bad habit, one which probably is a major contributor to pup mortality rates from automobiles.

When you reach the blind, you should place your dog with three considerations in mind:

(1) Can he see the action?

He should be sitting where he can see the ducks working. You can train him to do everything except look for the ducks. He must learn that by hunting, and he'll learn it much faster if he is sitting where he can see the action. A good spot is a platform attached to the blind. A dog sitting outside the blind will not flare ducks. If he's in a pit, put him high enough so he can peek over the top. The only objection I have to placing a dog outside a pit is the danger of muzzle blast deafening him or an excitable shooter blowing his head off.

The breaking dog is subject to muzzle blast.

Pup will learn to watch for ducks more quickly on open water than in timber, so consider making a water trip his first one.

(2) Does he have protection from the elements?

Place your dog where he's out of the water when he's not retrieving. Cold water soaks off body heat like a sponge, especially when he's sitting still in the water. I've seen a big tough Chesapeake nearly succumb to hypothermia simply because he insisted on staying in the water. If it's a cold windy day and you're pressing up behind a tree to get out of the wind, be sure to give pup a wind break too.

(3) Is he safe from the shooters?

Place him where he won't be in the blast cone of any shotguns. A few volleys of 12 gauge magnum right over his head will permanently deafen him.

He must be steady to shot or he might jump in front of someone's gun. If he's not steady, or he's been sitting in the kennel since last season, or if it's his first hunt, he's probably going to break a bit. Tie him up short so he can't break. But don't tie him to your belt; you might end up in the water or,

Black Swamp -
Cache River, Arkansas
Old Cypress Blind - 1947
(still in use today)

worse yet, fall forward with a loaded gun. Don't let pup go for your ducks with a choke chain collar around his neck. If he gets hung up on some brush because of the collar, you might not be able to get to him quickly enough.

After all the shooting is done, release pup to retrieve. If you do this the first couple of hunts, you'll probably not have any more trouble the rest of the season. It's the dog who occasionally gets away with misbehaving who becomes the chronic breaker and a problem.

One of the things that I have trouble with while hunting is a tendency to send pup too fast, i.e., just as the bird hits the water or earlier. When you start this, pup begins to expect to be released quickly and soon he will anticipate your moves. This usually develops into breaking.

A final point on pup's first hunt is to try to limit the number of shooters. If you put him in a blind with 12 guys shooting 3 inch magnums, he's going to have a tough time figuring out what is going on. The ideal first hunt for pup is over open water with one other person to shoot the ducks while you handle and pay attention to pup.

Taking pup with one good shot who can kill ducks on his first hunt will teach him that there really is a reason for that long, cold boat ride in the wind, and sitting in a little box above water for several hours.

In hot weather hunting, as for doves, the handler must be constantly aware of the possibility of heat stroke. Heat stroke is brought on by pup's body temperature rising too high for his cooling system to cope with.

Pup's cooling system consists of the mucous membranes of his mouth and throat. These are the only surfaces from which evaporation takes place. In other words, pup sweats only through his mouth and tongue.

This evaporation process is what sucks off the heat. The more body surface area that is wet and thus evaporating, the more heat is removed. This is the same principle upon which canvas water bags work.

To keep pup cool, wet down his whole body periodically. This is as important as giving him a drink of water. A caution on wetting him down, however. Don't put a wet dog in an enclosed space with restricted ventilation on a hot day. This will raise the humidity in that space, tremendously inhibiting evaporation. By slowing down evaporation, humidity slows down pup's cooling system.

The most dangerous conditions for heat strokes are encountered on hot, humid days with no wind. The symptoms are increased panting, vacant staring gaze, weakness, and a staggering gait. Some Labs will just keel over with no real warning signs especially if they are really hard goers. Immediately put the dog in cool water and get him to a vet as quickly as possible.

The best way to deal with heat strokes is to prevent them. Remember that pup is not smart enough to slow himself down. Keep him in the shade when he's not retrieving. Periodically wet him down. Have him in good

Make pup sit before you take the bird — it helps build character!

physical condition before hunting season arrives. Have him thin for hot weather and heavier for cold. If you're getting him in shape in the summer months, do your training in the early morning or late evenings, or work him in the water. Swimming is a great way to tone up your dog.

If pup's first season is successful as far as getting to retrieve a good number of ducks, the standard of control you maintain will stay with him for years of hunting to come.

If he's in good shape physically and has had a good training program, he'll have a good time and so will you.

This training program has been presented intentionally as fairly rigid and stereotyped. This is the pattern your relationship with pup should follow during his first season of hunting. There will be plenty of subsequent seasons for the relationship to mellow into the traditional picture of pup as a hunting companion. If you keep it tight and proper during the first season pup will retain his behavior as a civilized, controllable companion. If you get loose during that first season then you'll probably be fighting pup for control for subsequent seasons.

old Eastern Shore
Golden Eye

References and Useful Books for Further Reading

Campbell, William E., *Behavior Problems in Dogs*. Santa Barbara, American Veterinary Publications, 1975.

Fox, Dr. Michael W., *Understanding Your Dog*. New York, Coward, McCann and Geoghegan, 1972.

Fox, Dr. Michael W., *Canine Behavior,* Springfield, Charles C. Thomas, 1965.

Kersley, J.A., *Training the Retriever*. New York, Howell. 1971.

Koehler, W.R., *The Koehler Method of Open Obedience for Ring, Home and Field*. New York, Howell, 1978.

Lopez, Barry H., *Of Wolves and Men*. New York, Charles Scribner's Sons. 1978.

Mowat, Farley, *Never Cry Wolf*. Boston: Little, Brown. 1963.

Scott, J.P., *Animal Behavior*. Chicago, University of Chicago Press. 1972.

Scott, J.P. and Huller, J.L., *Genetics and Social Behavior of the Dog*. Chicago, University of Chicago Press. 1965.

Tarrant, Bill, *Hey Pup, Fetch It Up*. Scottsdale, Sun Trails. 1979.

Tortora, Daniel F., Ph.D., *Understanding Electronic Dog Training*. Tucson, Tri-Tronics. 1982.

Walters, D.L. and Ann, *Training Retrievers to Handle*. Olathe, Kansas, Interstate. 1979.

Walters, D.L., and Fowler, Ann, edited by, *Charles Morgan On Retrievers*. Stonington, VT, October House. 1974.

Wolters, Richard A., *Water Dog*. New York, E.P. Dutton. 1964.

TRAINING RULES
Introduction to Hunting

1. Know your dog's personality type and treat him accordingly. Observe pup during the training process and he'll tell you what type he is.

2. Give one command in normal tone and volume of voice. Don't shout and don't repeat commands.

3. Don't obtain response by threats; do it by conditioning the responses.

4. Develop habits through response conditioning and repetition, rather than by testing and correction.

5. Be decisive in what you are teaching pup, and give commands, not requests.

6. Don't indiscriminately reward pup with petting and/or praise. Save it for the times pup does something properly.

7. Don't try to accomplish too much too soon.

8. Be patient.

9. Be objective.

10. Above all, be consistent.

Touchdown!
Banded Greenhead Mallard
in
Backwater Slough

7 week old puppy,
1st water Retrieve~
'Music City's Jesse Jane~
OWNER: La Donna Crowe

Chapter 2 — Puppies
Problem Clinic — Q & A

1. **Q.** I have a 3 months old lab puppy who eats the bird when I throw it for him to retrieve and shows little interest in a dummy. How can I carry on with a retrieving program?

A. Bird eating in puppies can sometimes be brought on by poor training techniques. All puppies probably have some tendency to take that bird to the bushes and eat it. After all, that is the ancestral behavior from which the retrieving instinct is derived. What the trainer must do is deprive pup of the behavior path of going to the bushes with the bird while promoting an alternative, which is coming to the trainer. Yelling, threatening or chasing pup will deprive pup of the path back to the trainer, and leave him no place to go except the bushes, where he will probably eat the bird.

The promoting of the desired path of behavior can be accomplished through habit formation or through physical restraint with the checkcord. To do it by habit you simply let pup do his retrieving with a dummy or ball neither of which is likely to trigger the eating response.

A few weeks of retrieving dummies should establish the desired behavior sufficiently that you'll have no trouble with birds.

If, as in our present question, pup is already eating birds and isn't interested in dummies then the solution lies in physical restraint. Put the checkcord on pup, and use frozen birds for his retrieves. If you haul him in as soon as he picks up the bird then he won't have time to eat it. Four or five retrieves per day for two or three weeks should establish the retrieving behavior well enough to progress to a dummy with a bird wing taped to it. Also try the dummy in the water. Frequently a puppy that won't pick up a dummy on land will pick it up in the water.

2. **Q.** My 3 month old puppy won't retrieve in the water. What do I do?

A. If it's winter then wait till summer for the young pup's water work. If it's summer then put on a pair of shorts and walk in, calling pup with you. If he won't follow you in, then pull him gently in with the checkcord and plenty of petting. When he's feeling comfortable in the water then toss him 3 or 4 short retrieves in water shallow enough that he doesn't have to swim. As his confidence builds toss the dummy a bit further each time until he's swimming for it. Build up the distances gradually such that he's always successful.

3. **Q.** I have a 6 month old puppy who I got before I got your book. I've spent a lot of time on obedience training and he does great on heeling, sitting, staying and coming. However, he's not very interested in retrieving. What do you suggest?

A. You've done it backwards. You should have developed pup's natural qualities first, gotten him crazy to retrieve, and then superimpose the control behavior. The proper course of action would be to eliminate the control for several weeks. Just play with pup and try to get him interested in retrieving something, be it ball, sock, bird, old glove, etc. If you cannot get him to exhibit any interest in 2 or 3 weeks of this then get another pup. Sometimes a pup is genetically deficient in the retrieving instinct. If this is the case then no amount of training can put in what isn't there to begin with.

4. **Q.** My 4 month old puppy was doing great on the retrieving until 3 days ago when he just quit. What is the matter?

A. First take him to the vet and have him checked out. He may be sick. If he's well but quit retrieving then he's probably overworked and/or suffering from lack of success. A young pup tends to be short on endurance and it's easy to work him to the point of exhaustion when you're simply standing around throwing dummies while he's doing all the work. Also too much testing on hard retrieves where he fails to find the dummy can discourage him and dull his interest.

The solution is to let him sit in the kennel for a week and come back with a program of 4 or 5 retrieves per day, making them easy enough that he's always successful.

"The Great Masking Tape Robbery"
9 weeks old—
"Diamond in The Ruff"

5. **Q.** My three month old puppy has lots of enthusiasm and really charges out there on retrieves, but if he doesn't find the dummy fairly quickly, then he gives up and comes back without it. How can I increase his persistence?

A. You are probably training this trait into pup by making the retrieves too hard too early. The way to instill persistence in a young pup is through building his confidence through success. Set up his retrieves such that he always finds the dummy. In large part this consists of programming pup to use his eyes. He's born with a propensity to use his nose to find things but he needs a little help on the eye use. Use white or light colored dummies on a bare field, such that he can see them lying on the ground. You want to develop in pup the confidence that the dummy is always where he saw it fall. This will come as the habit of using his eyes becomes stronger over a period of several weeks. Keep the retrieves easy and don't expect an overnight cure.

drawing "Puppy Golden Retriever" "Bandit"

Fast Pitch, anyone?
"— 8 Week's Old —
Good Times Boss"

Chapter 3 — Relating to Your Pup
Problem Clinic — Q & A

1. **Q.** My two year old lab bit my 4 year old son last week. What can I do to prevent this happening again?

   A. My advice would be to give the dog to someone who doesn't have children. It was probably the child's fault that he was bitten. He undoubtedly did something to pup which triggered the defense response of biting. However, how do you insure that those same conditions won't occur again? Trying to keep child and pup separated would probably result in pup's being banished from the family and placed in relative isolation. This would probably make pup neurotic plus depriving you and the family of his companionship. Not a very good situation for either of you. Get another pup from stock showing less aggressiveness.

2. **Q.** My lab is trained and performs well for me but my wife can not control him. What can I do to improve this situation?

   A. There is not much you can do but there is something your wife can do. She can try to change her behavior relative to pup. First she should conduct pup through some obedience drills. This is not to teach pup the obedience but rather to condition him to respond to your wife. Further, when she wishes to obtain a response from pup she should project the attitude that she expects compliance. This attitude follows from issuing commands (tone, not volume) rather than requests.

   Additional improvement will come from refraining from soliciting affection from pup. Don't reward indiscriminately. Pet and praise pup for performing a commanded action.

   In short your wife should obtain some dominance in the relationship and consistently maintain it. Then pup's trained behavioral responses will be operative for her as well as for yourself.

133

3. **Q.** I work 5 days a week and don't have time to train my dog on week days. Can I effectively train him using only weekends?

A. Yes, but it will take a whole lot longer. I don't recommend trying to pack a week's worth of training into two days. Frankly, if you can't spare 15 minutes per day for pup then why take on the responsibility in the first place?

4. **Q.** My dog barks a lot in his kennel and my neighbors are complaining. Do you have an easy solution?

A. Barking in the kennel is frequently attributable to a lack of outlet for pup's energy and/or a lack of attention. Spending more time with him can frequently help alleviate the problem.

If the neighbors are really irate and you need a quick solution, then get pup a dog crate. During the time of day or night that the barking is most evident put pup and the crate in your house; this will probably break the chain of stimuli causing the barking. If he's still barking in the house and it's bothering you, put pup and the crate in basement or garage where the sound is muffled. When pup finds out that barking doesn't bring any attention then he'll quit.

5. **Q.** I've noticed that my pup, who is normally very responsive to commands, responds very poorly when I am petting him. Is this normal?

A. Three cheers for your powers of observation! It's quite normal for pup to not hear commands very well when you are petting him. Dogs are much more receptive to the sense of touch than to the sense of hearing. Petting or touching pup while giving a command is like putting in ear plugs.

"The Old Man", Rocky
FC-AFC IRON WOOD'S
12 Yr. Old Yellow

"INTENSITY"
BLACK LABRADOR
Male — 4 yrs. old.

Chapter 4 — When to Start Training Pup
Problem Clinic — Q & A

1. **Q.** I read a couple of books that recommend starting pup's training at a much earlier age than 6 months. What do you say about this?

A. I'm all for it, however, I prefer to call it development rather than training for the young puppy. Teach a puppy as much as you can, but teach as a game. The problem in training a very young puppy is with people. There are a lot of people who don't have the patience and dog sense to train a young puppy and keep it on the right note. The period from 6 weeks to 4 or 5 months of age is the time when pup is most open to learning but it is also the time when the margin for error in training is the least. The program I present is one which I think will be the most successful for the greatest number of dogs and the greatest number of people.

2. **Q.** I have a five year old dog. Is that too old to train?

A. No, that is not too old, especially if the dog is fairly tractable and has plenty of retrieving desire. On the other hand, if he's had five years of practice at running away, eating birds or other similar undesirable behaviors, he may reach retirement age before you complete the job.

3. **Q.** My pup is 6 months old and likes retrieving, however he's a bit shy of new situations and strange people.

A. I'm a little shy about strange people myself, so I wouldn't hold that against him. However, I would give him another month or two of exposure to different new situations, to build his confidence before beginning the formal training.

4. **Q.** I just acquired a 9 month old pup two weeks ago. Since duck season is coming up in 2 months, should I start his training immediately and try to get as much done as possible so I can take him?

A. No. Not unless you can figure out how to communicate the season dates to pup. Never let outside influences, even those as important as duck season, dictate your dog training schedule. Pup should dictate the dog training schedule. Don't try to go faster than pup will go. You should take him through the same development program that is prescribed for the young puppy (under 6 months) prior to beginning his formal training.

FC/AFC
Wild Fire of
River View —
Golden Retriever

Lab on Dog ramp
in duck Blind
"TACOS
Burrito Supreme"

Chapter 5 — Obedience
Problem Clinic — Q & A

1. **Q.** My dog does great on obedience in the backyard but anywhere else he becomes very deaf. Where did I go wrong?

   A. You shortcut his obedience training and probably inadvertently taught him that distractions were sufficient excuse for disobedience. He should have had more drill, repetition, and conditioning before he left the backyard and he should have been under physical control (the checkcord) when you gave the first commands in the presence of distraction. You went to the field with a partially trained pup and gave commands that you were not in a position to enforce. Thus you communicated to pup that the behavioral limits of the backyard didn't apply in the field.

   The solution is more drill, repetition and conditioning in the backyard. If you go to the field before pup is reliable then use either a checkcord or a closed mouth.

2. **Q.** I put my 7 month old pup through the obedience program and he does great when he's wearing the checkcord. When he's not wearing it he runs away. What's the solution?

   A. Obviously, you've taken the checkcord away too soon and allowed pup to learn that he can run away when he's not wearing it. The solution is to religiously put the checkcord on pup every time he's unconfined. Since he's now more educated than you wish, he'll need to keep wearing it a much longer time. You don't want even one more occurrence of the circumstances which trigger the running away response.

   Additionally try to make being in the immediate vicinity to you more pleasant for pup. Pet him a lot more, etc. This in conjunction with the habit produced by continually wearing the checkcord will over a period of time produce a pup who won't run away.

3. **Q.** My dog has been obedience trained and does quite well when he's close to me. However, past thirty yards he becomes increasingly disobedient, proportionate to the distance even when wearing a checkcord.

A. The answer here is basically the same as for the previous question. You're attempting too much too soon. By testing him at a distance before his responses are consistent enough you are telegraphing to pup your lack of control for that distance.

Go back to obedience drills and be quite a stickler for compliance. When you start letting pup get a bit sloppy in close then you are issuing an invitation for disobedience at a distance. Then put pup through the conditioned retrieve process. This tends to have a dramatic effect on pup's compliance. It tends to channel excess energy into the act of retrieving and delivering the bird. This process could easily take care of your distance problem. If it doesn't then go to a longer checkcord and go out and catch and correct pup a few times. When he knows you're willing and able to come out there then his obedience will improve at a distance.

yellow lab with
cock pheasant—

4. **Q.** I try to bring pup out of his kennel under control but he frequently dodges past me and then won't come because he knows I'm going to put the checkcord on him. What should I do?

A. Don't rely on your ability to grab pup as he comes thundering out of the kennel. As a matter of fact, don't let him come thundering out of the kennel. That's not exactly controlled behavior. You go in the kennel, being careful to not allow him to dodge past you, and attach the checkcord there. Then walk pup out at heel.

5. **Q.** When I give pup his happy dummies he sometimes takes off with one and it takes quite a bit of yelling to get him back. What would you do about this?

A. If there is the slightest chance that pup may deviate from returning straight with the happy dummy, don't gamble. Snap on a 100 ft. checkcord, keeping the other end in your hand or under your foot. Use this, and not commands to get him back. You'll have a tough time establishing obedience if you begin and end each training session with disobedience.

young Black Duck

Chapter 6 — The Conditioned Retrieve
Problem Clinic — Q & A

1. **Q.** My dog eats birds and drops frozen birds that he can't eat (usually 10 feet out in the pond). He also spits dummies out as soon as they touch his mouth. Should I get rid of him?

   A. If he runs with enthusiasm and purpose to get that bird to eat then he's salvageable. If he's young and the bird eating is not an ingrained habit then the conditioned retrieve process will probably transform him into a dog. He certainly sounds birdy. He just hasn't received the proper guidance on what to do with the bird after he gets it.

   If he's 3 years old and just polished off his 100th bird, then I'd try another pup.

2. **Q.** I've started my pup on the conditioned retrieve and have progressed to lesson 6, but am not happy with pup's progress. His response is still slow and his attitude that of sulleness. I've been gradually increasing the intensity of the pinch but it hasn't helped.

   A. Some pups are going to initially respond to this process with sulleness. You're problem may lie in the gradualness of increase of intensity. If it's too gradual some pups will gradually adapt to the slowly increasing discomfort. You'll end up using more force than you really would have needed had you changed tactics. If you've got a pup that isn't improving, i.e. getting snappier, with a gradual increase then give him a sudden sharp increase to snap him out of that behavior pattern. When you are getting snappy responses, then lighten up.

3. **Q.** I've started my pup on the conditioned retrieve process and he's doing quite well. However, I really have to pull to get the dowel out of his mouth. Is there a remedy for this?

   A. Never pull on the dowel to remove it from pup's mouth. This will merely cause him to hold on tighter. The remedy is to grasp the dowel and blow forcefully on pup's nose as if you're blowing out a candle. This will cause some to release the dowel. If this doesn't work, then reach back and pinch his flank at the point his hind leg joins his torso. This will cause him to open his mouth. Use the command "LEAVE IT" or "DROP" in conjunction with this action. After enough repetitions, he'll respond to the command alone.

4. **Q.** I can't seem to get pup going on the transition from table to ground. He was pretty stubborn on the ear pinch but I finally got through to him. However on the ground it is a different story. How do I get consistent response on the ground?

   A. You probably blew it on the introduction to the ear pinch. There is a strong tendency to pinch harder if you don't get an immediate response. This is not necessary and some pups, if the initial pinching is too rough will be scared and freeze up. Give the initial pinches just hard enough to cause discomfort and give pup time to find the appropriate escape path which is the fetch. You've time; there is no need to get rough. If a few minutes of a discomforting pinch doesn't induce pup to fetch, then open his mouth and stick the dummmy in. Repeat this several times before resorting to a harder pinch.

   However if the mistake is made, here's how to salvage it. Put pup back on the table for several sessions with the toe pinch. Then we'll transfer to the stick you used for obedience. Sit pup on one end of the table and a dummy at the other. Command "FETCH" and start tapping him with the stick. The tapping should be of moderate intensity. We want to make pup uncomfortable, not beat him up. When he starts to move give him a light pinch so that the fetch response will follow. We're making it uncomfortable for pup to stay where he is and providing the escape path which is fetching the dummy. Don't worry about how fast he does it. After several sessions when the escape response is firmly established we can shape it or speed it up by increasing intensity of tapping. Don't try to do it all in one session. We want to do all this without scaring pup. Watch those ears and tail.

   When pup is responding well to the stick then try the transition to the ground again.

5. **Q.** I've taken my dog through your training program and he performs flawlessly on ducks and pigeons. I took him dove hunting last week and he'd pick them up and bring them back only part way before spitting them out.

   A. He needs a little remedial work on the conditioned retrieve. Some dogs don't like to carry doves, especially in hot weather. Give him a couple of sessions on the table with doves and then one or two on the ground. The next time he regresses in the field, an ear pinch or two should straighten him out. Also make sure you're not allowing him to get over heated. A bird in the mouth interferes with pup's cooling system.

STUMP BLIND (CYPRUS)
Reelfoot Lake, Tennessee
FOR DIVER HUNTING

Chesapeake Bay
Retriever — "Gal"
1983

Chapter 7 — Steadying
Problem Clinic — Q & A

1. **Q.** Why should pup be so steady? Don't you overdo it a bit?

   A. The pup that is not super steady in a training situation will probably break with the added excitement of the hunting situation. The breaking generally leads down a predictable path from bad to worse. First pup starts breaking on the splash of the fallen bird. Then he goes on, to breaking on just the sound of the gun, and finally to breaking when ducks are working. This last step greatly increases the chances of pup being permanently deafened by muzzle blast, or worse, accidentally shot. Additionally this erosion of steadiness will contribute to the breakdown of his other control behaviors and he'll be well on the way to becoming a real pain to take hunting.

2. **Q.** How great an affect does an occasional success at breaking have on the steadying process.?

   A. This is hard to quantify, but I will say that an occasional success has a tremendously degrading effect on the steadying process. The occasional success is equivalent to a variable schedule of reinforcement for breaking. Behavior learned by this process is the most resistant to extinction. Therefore, it will greatly increase either the time required for or the force required for the steadying process.

3. **Q.** I've always thought that sending a dog fast on his marked retrieves would make him mark better. Is this true?

   A. No. For the pup who is a bit slow or lacking in enthusiasm, sending fast is a great way to build up speed and desire for the bird, and should be used for this. However, it doesn't improve marking in the pup who already exhibits plenty of go power. If anything a lack of steadiness will make the eager pup's marking worse. He's more prone to watch the bird down and remembers it location when he's sitting still as opposed to jumping and bouncing around.

4. Q. Do you really need to use birds in the steadying process?

A. Yes. You want to develop the habit with dummies so as to increase the odds of success. However pup's not steady till the habit is built up enough to withstand the extreme distractions of the hunting situation. You can't get a very close approximation of these hunting conditions without using birds.

5. Q. Pup is steady and I've been running him on lots of double marked retrieves. He sometimes gives up on the hunt for the memory bird and goes back to where he picked up the first one. My field trial friends call this switching and punish their dogs for it. Should I do the same?

A. It's natural for pup to switch. We've programmed it into him to a certain extent with repetition on lining drills and sight blinds and by repeating marks. In these exercises he's being sent back to the same place he just picked up a dummy. Therefore, you can expect it to carry over a bit to double marked retrieves.

As to punishing pup for switching, I'm against it. I've tried it both ways, punishing and not punishing. Both seem to be equally effective. I prefer to simply let him find out that he doesn't get the bird when he switches. Just help him out on the memory bird and then repeat the double. As his confidence builds he'll become more proficient and the frequency of switching will decrease.

Punishing for switching merely gives pup something else to worry about which interferes with his confidence. His lack of confidence is probably what caused him to give up the hunt on the memory bird and switch in the first place. Punishing just compounds the problem.

Black Duck Decoy —
Solid Cork — (Over Sized)
Typical Eastern Shore —

Chapter 8 — Duck Blinds and Hand Signals
Problem Clinic — Q & A

1. **Q.** I've been doing the casting drill with pup and he frequently goes the wrong way. I'm having to yell at him a lot to stop him and he's becoming hesitant about taking a cast. I'm afraid he'll start balking. What should I do?

   A. Congratulations on recognizing a developing problem. The essence of dog training is to recognize an approaching problem and solve it before it gets a good start.

   The solution is the checkcord. When pup goes the wrong way, stop him with a whistle blast and hand on checkcord. This give you two-for-one. You're stopping him without the yelling, which is what's worrying him and causing the hesitation. Additionally you are reinforcing stopping on the whistle. When you've stopped him pull that dummy out of your back pocket, toss it the right way and give him another cast.

2. **Q.** I've tried to start pup on the casting drill and he won't take a cast. He wants to come to me before going for the dummy. How do I sove this?

   A. You've got him a little too steady. He's so programmed to go only from your side, that he's afraid to launch from a spot 10 feet away from you. Go back and do a few sessions on the table and then try again, initially with the very short casts of about 3 feet. Sometimes a little HUP HUP with the cast will loosen him up.

3. **Q.** I've got pup started on your triple line drill and he's beginning to balk quite a bit. What should I do?

   A. You're probably trying to go too fast with pup. I assume that the balking is a result of your stopping pup and calling him back frequently for taking the wrong line. Too much of this will generally cause balking. Either you're going faster than pup's confidence or your own motor skills are not precise enough to communicate to put the small angular differences in lines. The solution is to move closer, increasing the angle between lines until pups confidence returns. Then decrease the angle more gradually, giving pup time to build confidence and yourself time to build the motor skills required of the handler.

4. **Q.** I can't get pup to line up under my hand. He ducks his head away. What can I do?

A. Pup is probably ducking away from your hand for one of two reasons. You may be placing your hand such that you are blocking pup's vision and he's ducking to the side to be able to see out past it. The other reason for ducking may be nervousness about that hand. You may have been slapping him too much with it. In either case give him a lot of short lining drills with white dummies. Get your hand out forward and further above his head where it's not bothering him so much. You want him thinking "out-there" instead of thinking about your hand.

Your decoy string is all he needs

"slidin In"
Paul Cannasback
1982
"Bear Creek"

Chapter 9 — Water Training
Problem Clinic — Q & A

1. **Q.** My dog is a great water retriever. He hits the water hard and does some pretty long retrieves. He has, however, one small fault. On his return with the bird he stops out in the water just out of reach and plays with the bird. It usually takes 10 or 15 minutes of coaxing to get him to bring the bird to me. Since this is his only fault can you recommend a remedy so that I don't have to take him through your entire training program?

A. I doubt that this is his only fault, but assuming that it is, I'll give you the quick fix. That would be to work him on a 30 foot checkcord and give him 25 foot retrieves in the water, keeping one end of the checkcord in hand. Pull him on in when he stops to play. When he's coming on in voluntarily lengthen the retrieves but let him keep trailing a checkcord as a reminder for several more weeks.

The quick fix solution is not the best way to go. It usually leads to an unending cycle of quick fixes such that pup is never really trained and controllable. For example what if the pulling with the checkcord causes pup to spit out the bird and leave it out in the water beyond reach? If he hasn't been through the conditioned retrieve process then you've got another problem as bad as the first.

You'd be much better off to go ahead and train pup properly now. Then you can enjoy him as a hunting companion for the next seven or eight years instead of arguing with him for the next seven or eight years.

2. **Q.** I've introduced pup properly to the water and he goes in with great enthusiasm. However when he gets there he can't swim right. I've tried heavy dummies and that didn't solve the problem. Do you have any other suggestions?

A. Check the depth of your pond. If the water is shallow enough for pup to keep his hind feet on the bottom with his head above water then, he may never quit flailing with the front feet. You may need deeper water. If depth isn't the problem then you have two choices. You can go in with pup and hold his collar while supporting his belly to keep him level in the water. Then move him along gently till he's swimming properly. Alternatively you can get in a boat and pull pup along in the water with a rope attached to his collar. Paddle the boat just a bit faster than pup can swim. The resulting pull on his neck will level him out and he'll learn to swim properly.

3. **Q.** My Lab retrieves on land with style and enthusiasm, however she literally walks into the water on water retrieves. I've given her lots of short water retrieves on pigeons and ducks for the past two weeks, and have seen no improvement. What would you do?

    A. If she has the retrieving desire on land then it should be there for water also. She has either a physical or emotional aversion to water. By physical, I mean something about the water may be causing her discomfort. Take her to the vet and get her checked out. Have him X-Ray her hip and shoulder joints. Pulling through the mud at the edge of the lake can be painful on abnormal hip or shoulder joints.

    If the problem isn't of physical origin then it must be emotional, a past bad association. Enough short water retrieves on birds will get her out of it.

4. **Q.** I tried to start my lab on your water handling pattern last week and he started refusing to go in the water. What should I do?

    A. You've probably tried to accelerate the program. I would guess that your pup's balking is stemming from too much harassment (yelling) to get him to stop on the whistle. Go back to marks and sight blinds in the water for a couple of weeks. Meanwhile go back and run more of the land handling pattern to get pup's whistle stopping more automatic. Then try again.

5. **Q.** I lost my temper last week and punished pup on a water training session when I shouldn't have. Now he frequently refuses to go on marks. What should I do?

    A. You have several choices. You can give him lots of short water retrieves with birds to build his confidence back up. You could also put him in the kennel for a week or two to build up his enthusiasm. Or you can condition him to go on water retrieves.

    This conditioning should only be attempted when two requirements are fulfilled.

    Pup must have previously been retrieving confidently in the water and he must have been through the conditioned retrieve process.

    Put a checkcord on pup and sit him at the water's edge. Toss 3 dummies 3 feet out in the water. Don't let pup retrieve them voluntarily. Grasping the checkcord one foot from the collar, give the command "FETCH" and begin tapping pup with the stick. The tapping is to make it uncomfortable for pup to remain where he is. You're firm grasp on

The Big Honker

croul bus
Feet Down —
Safty Off —

the checkcord is to block all avenues of escape except that toward the dummy. We preprogrammed this escape response toward a dummy with the conditioned retrieve. When pup does move toward the dummy, you want it to be his decision so do not pull him toward it with the checkcord. The checkcord is simply to prevent an escape route in any direction other than toward the water and the dummy. The tapping with the stick should be moderate; it should be strong enough to make him uncomfortable but not so strong as to panic him. As you tap and pup becomes uncomfortable he's going to try to move away from the spot in which he's sitting. He'll try to move back away from the water first and then to either side but the firmly grasped checkcord will block these avenues and pup will finally take the proper path into the water to the dummy. Accomplish this process 3 times for the 3 dummies tossed out. The trick here is to keep the tapping at the same moderate intensity. Don't get impatient and overdo it. The steady moderate tapping if kept up is going to cause pup to move eventually, and he'll finally take the right escape path. The duration of tapping will decrease greatly with each repetition of the response.

After he's picked up those first three dummies, toss them out again about 6 feet from the bank and repeat the process. Then do it for 3 dummies at 9 feet from the bank, and that will be sufficient for the first lesson. Come back tomorrow and do 3 more sets of three beginning at 9 feet and extending the distance 3 feet for each successive set of 3 retrieves. The third session should be conducted in like manner beginning at 15 feet and extending to 21 feet.

These three sessions should be enough to program pup against balking at the water. If they are not, then give him a few more.

Remember this is absolutely not the way to introduce pup to the water. This process must be attempted only after pup has built up some confidence in the water and after he's been through the conditioned retrieve process. This conditioning of the water retrieve is a remedy for poor training techniques on the part of the trainer.

Mason Challenge Grade
Merganser Decoy

Chapter 11 — Introduction to Hunting
Problem Clinic Q & A

1. **Q.** Should a hunting dog live in the house?

A. Yes, by all means, within certain limitations. For several weeks prior to and during duck season, pup should live outside so that he is acclimatized to the cold. Remember he doesn't have waders and a big goose down parka to put on for the duck hunt.

The other objection is aimed at people. When pup is living in the house, the boss tends to get loose on control, and pup tends to do the same. This can result in some people losing their temper in the field and punishing pup for their own lack of consistency.

However many people don't have this shortcoming and for them it's great to have pup in the house. He can be an enjoyable companion and family dog as well as a worker.

2. **Q.** Can my friends borrow my dog and hunt him without detracting from his level of training?

A. That depends on the friend and what sort of dog person he is. I wouldn't loan pup out until he was past his first season. The first one is still a learning and training time and you want pup to learn what you expect of him; not what your friend expects of him.

Personally, I don't think I'd let my pup go hunting with a friend who didn't want me along also. He'll probably take all pup's money in the poker game.

3. **Q.** My lab had a great first duck season and picked up over 100 ducks. During this, his second season, he's become gunshy. He still retrieves the ducks, but everytime I shoot he runs around behind the blind.

A. It sounds like you let him get a bit loose on the steadiness for his second season. He's been out front of the guns a few times at the wrong time and received a dose of muzzle blast. The ducking behind the blind is an attempt to escape the muzzle blast he now associates with shooting.

Reinforce the steadiness and reintroduce the shotgun so he can learn again that it won't hurt him when he's in the proper place.

4. **Q.** I've put my lab through your training program including the conditioned retrieve. He performs flawlessfly on ducks but tends to be hardmouthed on doves. What is the cure?

A. Feed him a little before the hunt. Some pups exhibit a hard mouth simply from being hungry. If further action is necessary, then everytime he crunches a dove, take if from him and put it on the ground. Grasping his colar, administer an ear pinch with the command "FETCH." He would probably fetch without the ear pinch but you want him to know that you made him pick it up. Hold him off the bird if necessary to get in the pinch. This awareness by pup that you made him fetch the bird reinforces your ownership of it. This will damp out the hardmouth behavior.

5. **Q.** After pup has been through your training program how often does he need work to stay sharp?

A. That will vary with the nature of the individual dog in conjunction with the relationship which you maintain with him. If he's a fairly tractable dog and you maintain a consistent dominant relationship, then he'll need nearly no subsequent training.

The best rule is to cast an objective eye upon pup periodically and note any developing deficiencies. Then go back and do a little maintenance conditioning with the appropriate drill, i.e. obedience drill for heeling, sitting, staying, and coming; handling pattern for blinds and whistle stopping; etc.

Sailing Greenhead looking for Company~

Dear reader,

Since 1977, Wildrose Kennels has been dedicated to providing the most effective, most gentle training program for retrievers. I have worked with the best trainers in America and England to produce a gundog-training philosophy and program that is radically different, that is effective, and that is gentle to the canine students.

Wildrose Kennels offers this training course to your dog. Call us if you would like to reserve a position for your dog in the next class, or for further information.

Wildrose Kennels also breeds superior Labrador puppies. We import numerous dogs from England and have combined the best of American and British breeding to produce the gundog of superior quality. Our gundogs are bred to be equally talented at being a gundog or being a housedog. We breed for good looks, calm temperament, intelligence, diligence at working, and tractability. We produce Labradors that will do a great job at retrieving your ducks or raising your children. We normally have black, yellow, or chocolate puppies available. We also have a superb dog-training videotape entitled, *Retriever Training, A Better Way*. This video gives you the pictures to make your training task easier.

For further information call or write:

WILDROSE KENNELS
P.O. Box 281
Grand Junction, TN 38039
Tel. (901) 764 - 2495

We welcome your inquiries.

Sincerely,

Robert Milner